ECONOMIC THEORY BY TAUSSIG, YOUNG, AND CARVER AT HARVARD

RESEARCH IN THE HISTORY OF ECONOMIC THOUGHT AND METHODOLOGY

Founding Editor: Warren J. Samuels

Series Editors: Jeff E. Biddle, Ross B. Emmett and Marianne Johnson

Recent Volumes:

RESEARCH IN THE HISTORY OF ECONOMIC THOUGHT
AND METHODOLOGY   VOLUME 28-C

ECONOMIC THEORY BY TAUSSIG, YOUNG, AND CARVER AT HARVARD

EDITED BY

MARIANNE JOHNSON

Department of Economics
University of Wisconsin-Oshkosh, Oshkosh, WI, USA

WARREN J. SAMUELS

Department of Economics
Michigan State University, East Lansing, MI, USA

Emerald

United Kingdom – North America – Japan
India – Malaysia – China

Emerald Group Publishing Limited
Howard House, Wagon Lane, Bingley BD16 1WA, UK

First edition 2010

British Library Cataloguing in Publication Data
A catalogue record for this book is available from the British Library

ISBN: 978-0-85724-063-7
ISSN: 0743-4154 (Series)

Emerald Group Publishing
Limited, Howard House,
Environmental Management
System has been certified by
ISOQAR to ISO 14001:2004
standards

Awarded in recognition of
Emerald's production
department's adherence to
quality systems and processes
when preparing scholarly
journals for print

INVESTOR IN PEOPLE

CONTENTS

PART I

CORRESPONDENCE BETWEEN FRANK H. KNIGHT, WALTER B. SMITH, AND F. TAYLOR OSTRANDER, 1933–1937

Written in Part and Edited in Part by Warren J. Samuels

Taylor Ostrander received his BA from Williams College in 1932. He spent the academic year 1932–1933 studying at Oxford University. In the academic year 1933–1934, he attended courses at the University of Chicago. He returned to Williams College as an Instructor for 1934–1935. In 1935 Ostrander went to Washington, DC, to work with Aaron Director at the Treasury (Samuels, 2004).

GROUP ONE: WALTER BUCKINGHAM SMITH AND FRANK H. KNIGHT

Ostrander went to Chicago at the urging of his Williams professor Walter B. Smith who had studied with Frank Knight at Chicago in the early 1920s. He took four courses from Knight: the history of economic thought, economic theory, current tendencies, and economics from an institutional standpoint (his notes taken in these courses have appeared in volume 22B and 23B in this series). At the beginning of the academic year in which he was a graduate student at Chicago, Ostrander's major professor at Williams, Walter Buckingham Smith, wrote Knight introducing Ostrander to him. Ostrander did not know of this exchange of letters until he read a draft of this piece that I had sent him. The letters are useful in regard to Knight's legendary pessimism and candor.

Economic Theory by Taussig, Young, and Carver at Harvard
Research in the History of Economic Thought and Methodology, Volume 28-C, 1–9
Copyright © 2010 by Emerald Group Publishing Limited
All rights of reproduction in any form reserved
ISSN: 0743-4154/doi:10.1108/S0743-4154(2010)000028C002

September 30, 1933

Dear Professor Knight:

I am writing to tell you that we are sending you a graduate student named Ostrander from Williams. To a considerable extent he is coming to the University of Chicago on my recommendation. I particularly want him to work with you and with Professor Viner and with Professor Douglas. I'll be interested to see what you do with him. In my opinion he has "promise."

Mr. Ostrander graduated here in 1932 and spent last year in Oxford. He seems to have survived a year at Oxford. Usually a year or two there is pretty hard for an American to get over. Ostrander, contrary to the usual rule, seems to have benefited rather than deteriorated under the direction of his English tutors.

Ostrander is much interested in theoretical economics. My hope is that you will be able to do for him what I think you have a unique capacity to do. I hope that you can make him see economic theory not as a body of neat precepts nor as dogmas that one must learn but rather as a critical philosophizing about the categories. Needless to say, I'm not trying to tell you what you should teach your students. I'm merely telling you that I think that Ostrander is an intelligent enough person to understand you if you do in the class room what you used to do when I listened to you. He will understand; and he won't reproach you if your lectures don't enable him to get up a good note book.

I spent the year before last in Berkeley at the University there and got very well acquainted with your brother M.M. Needless to say, that was one of the most valuable things that happened to me while I was there. I don't understand why some eastern institution does not make M.M. a good offer and take him away from Berkeley where he is highly esteemed by all but sadly overlooked on pay-day.

Do you ever come east? If you do we would be delighted to entertain you and Mrs. Knight here in Williamstown. I would like ever so much to be able to talk with you about economics. If you should come this way you may be sure that we would be very glad to see you.

Sincerely yours,

[signed] Walter Smith

October 5, 1933

Dear Smith:

(I don't know how I ought to address you, but can't bring myself to "Professor" you, even though you did me.) I was just going to write you anyway when your letter came in the mail. Your man Ostrander arrived last week, and I had a couple of hours' talk with him, business being slack on the first day of registration. He impressed me quite favorably. One thing he may have gotten in Oxford or in part from his eastern bringing up (we have a Princeton boy who is fully as bed [sic]) is an extremely deferential air which is embarrassing to me. I very much appreciate your comments, and I am, of course, quite set up at your sending him to us as against Harvard.

By all means, any possible opportunity to get together and talk about economics. I am so depressed that it is really serious for my work. I have to fight the conviction that anything in any degree fundamental is impossible, hopeless. On one hand I agree very largely with the "rebels" that rationalistic economics doesn't amount to a terrible lot, even if it were sound. But on the other hand the little that it does have to say about social relations and problems seems to me as peculiarly fundamental as it is limited in scope. But I suspect that man, in his well known capacity of "political animal," is an inveterate romanticist, and will never see things in balance or perspective. He will either be a rationalist to the point of romanticism – the "Enlightenment" attitude – or else insist on scorning all fundamentals and transforming the world by wish[ful] thinking or some magic formula.

I wonder what you think about current developments. I hope it may partly be due to a run-down physical condition, but actually my feeling is that we are seeing from day to day the "finish" of all we have educated ourselves to call the principal cultural fruits of western civilization. What gripes me is less this fact than the fact that I cannot rationally oppose the abolition of liberty and [the] establishment of tyranny. I feel that the regime of liberty has been a failure, or an experiment with negative results, that it has shown the incapacity of large masses of people to reach any sound conclusion by thinking and discussion – indeed the inevitability of their ending up by selling out to some hero-prophet. If this is the wrong view of events, I wish you would give me any possible help in reaching a view in which my own kind of person and of activity would have any place. I wonder if your failure to write may be based on a feeling similar to this one of my own, which is making it increasingly difficult for me to pretend to try to fan the wi[nd] of culture history into a new direction with a hen feather of words. Indeed, it is making it take an actual moral struggle a good deal of the time to open the door and go into an economics classroom and hold forth.

Sincerely,

Frank H. Knight

November 24, 1933

Dear FH:

Thank you ever so much for your letter about Ostrander. You will be interested to know that Ostrander writes with the very greatest enthusiasm for your course. I am sure that you are doing him a lot of good. Before the year is over I would be interested to have your opinion of him and of his capacities to undertake the arduous job of being an economist. He has seemed promising to me. If this promise seems not to be fulfilled in your opinion, I should feel disposed to tell him so and urge him to resume his plans for going to the Harvard Law School.

Your remarks about being depressed over the apparent disillusion of the existing economic order I very much sympathize with. Not only am I troubled about that but I am also very much troubled about the intellectual confusion and the lack of good sportsmanship on the part of the better trained economists these days. President Roosevelt seems to me to be willing to listen to reasonable and constructive suggestions and he has shown an extraordinary disposition to do some social experimenting. In the face of this extraordinary state of affairs it seems to me that the great body of well trained economists has contented themselves with growling quietly to one another and saying nothing in public. From the standpoint of maintaining one's prestige that is in some ways the wise policy for it enables one to say "I told you so" when things in the world of business fact go wrong. It does seem to me, however, that under the circumstances economists ought to make their position known, that is[,] to point out where they think the existing policies are leading, the important and possibly conflicting goals of different lines of economic policy and certain long run changes in the set up of our legal economic structure. If the economists can't do that much then it seems to be that they are confessing that their field is in such a state of intellectual confusion that it is practically worthless, or else they are confessing that they are a timid lot of thin-blooded academics who have no right to object if this country is run by the Babbitts.

This letter comes to you to find out if there is any possibility of starting a movement or making the opinion of the economists heard. Personally I think we ought to speak out or else publicly admit that the study and teaching of economics is a racket.

Sincerely yours,

[signed] Walter Smith

GROUP TWO: F. TAYLOR OSTRANDER AND FRANK H. KNIGHT

Ostrander had left the University of Chicago in 1934 to teach at Williams College and in 1935 went with Aaron Director to Washington, DC. Thus, in January 1937, Knight writes to him there concerning a book by Lewis Mumford that Ostrander had read in conjunction with Knight's course on Economics from an Institutionalist Standpoint. Ostrander had prepared a review of the book, *Technics and Civilization*, which was published in the *Journal of Political Economy*, the journal published by the economics department at Chicago. In a memorandum to me (October 22, 2009), Ostrander wrote that "Knight did not suggest to me back in 1934 or 1935 that I write a review of Mumford's book for JPE [and] Knight did not write to me in 1937 'relative to' the JPE review [as I had written, with incomplete information, in the draft of this piece]. In fact, Knight did not recall in 1937 that I had ever written such a review; if he had, he would have looked up the review then in 'his' JPE, instead of writing me in 1937."

January 23, 1937

Dear Ostrander:

The last time I gave the course in Institutional 1 Economics (I think it was), you gave a report on Lewis Munford's Technics and Civilization which impressed me considerably. In fact, you about convinced me that it wouldn't be worth the time and effort to read the book, and under the pressure of this and that, I never even looked into it until the last few days. Now I find it extremely interesting. It was my recollection that your paper or at least note was left here, but I can't find it. Do you have any kind of a draft or outline, which you could refer to, or would you mind writing me anything you can remember about your general line of criticism? I should appreciate it very much. I hope you are well and prosperous, and will get back some time to finish your work here.

 Cordially yours,

[signed] Frank H. Knight

February 10, 1937

Dear Mr. Knight:

I am sorry to have delayed this long in answering your letter about Mumford's book. I wish I had time to reread it and to report to you my present impressions. Not having the time to do that just now, I will only set down my opinions as I recall them from the summer of 1934, when I read the paper in your seminar. I did not leave any copy of that paper at the University, and, on going over the copy I have, find [it] far too verbose to send on to you. I did, however, have a short review of the book in the June 1935 issue of the J.P.E. and still hold substantially the same opinion of the book.

For the sake of comparison, I looked up today the only other journal reviews I could find. Mr. B.A. Thresher, in the *A. E. R.* (Volume 24, page 542) agreed that the author is essentially an artist, and that the book is extremely weak "when dealing with economic and political forces," but he was happy to find the attempt made to approach social studies along such lines. Allan Wallis' father, in *The Annals* (Volume 175, September 1934, p. 261) said that Mumford had a "poet's conception" and that *"Technics and Civilization* is a poem," but he held that many elements in the book contribute to our understanding of the machine age. As I will indicate below, my own feeling is that

I will summarize some of my more specific criticisms of the book:

1. *Mumford has not contributed anything to new scholarship*: his only sources are the more popular works of Sombart, Weber, etc., and his class notes of Bradford's and Geddes' lectures.

2. *There is an impossible eclecticism in his use of these secondary sources.* No one can properly combine in a single consistent philosophy the diverse attitudes of Sombart and

Marx, Veblen and D. H. Lawrence, Weber and Howard Scott, etc. Mumford does not seem to face this problem, or else he does not realize that the "cultural eras" described by these various "Institutionalists" are highly inconsistent with each other.

3. *There is throughout the book an aesthetic subjectivism*, without facing any of the problems implicit in such an approach, that places it outside the realm of serious works in social science. Spengler at least put forth a philosophy of the subjective approach (in the Preface to "Das Untergang") and Sombart has written a whole book to explain his method.

4. *The "Institutionalist" method of "philosophizing about history" is carried to a rare extreme*, surpassed, probably, only by Spengler. The evasions of common sense and good scholastic technique, necessary for the delineation of all "culture eras" is likewise carried to an extreme. What actual historical justification is there for the separation between the "Eotechnic" and the "Paleotechnic" eras? That greatest vice of the "Institutionalist" method, reading ideologic purpose into the course of history, is, again, present in this work in an extreme form. Although Mumford makes much of the anthropomorphic tendency of modern culture and of capitalism which read reality into the unreal and imaginary concepts of time, space, efficiency, and profits, he does not blanche at the obvious anthropomorphic quality of a "cultural era" which has not only an unreal beginning and end in time, an imagined pervasive and central theory and essence, but also a "goal" towards which all things operate.

5. *There is not even an elementary concept of the economic problem.* Some of the worst work in the book is in connection with the "new" concepts of production and consumption and the substitution of "energy efficiency" for "profit efficiency."

6. The acceptance of "Planning" as the solution of all evils shows an incredible *simple faith in the expert*. There is no mention of the problems connected with the introduction of "Planning" into a democracy.

I will be very interested to learn your opinion of the book and hope you will find time to drop me a word or two about your final reaction. I should like to know whether you have been "converted" to my approach or whether I have missed the point.

I am no longer with the Income Tax Study but am doing research in "International monetary problems" under Dr. Harry D. White, along with Glasser, Spiegel and Schmidt. I am planning to take the "Finance" examination in May and to return to the University for a quarter sometime to prepare for the Theory "General."

With best wishes,

F.T.O

February 25, 1937

My dear Ostrander:

Thanks very much for your letter regarding the Mumford book. It certainly confirms my recollected impression of your report in class. All the same, I found parts of it quite interesting where I dipped in, and think I'll dip in some more before consigning it to oblivion. What you say may all be true and yet the book may have some value for students if used under proper warning. I had myself noticed that his comments in the bibliography show a complete lack of critical attitude, and presumably of critical capacity. I am sorry you went to so much trouble, as I was only thinking you might have at hand some notes or what not calling attention to particular egregiousnesses in the work, I mean citing pages or sections.

I hope you are liking [sic] your work. You seem to have quite a Chicago group. I am afraid if I had a job which I liked and which paid more money than teaching at least until "when, as, and if" one gets pretty high up, the prospects of the teaching profession as I see them would not make me feel in a terrible hurry to make great sacrifices and get back into apprentice work in that line.

Cordially yours,

[signed] Frank H. Knight

OSTRANDER'S REVIEW IN THE JOURNAL OF POLITICAL ECONOMY, JUNE 1935

Technics and Civilization, by Lewis Mumford. New York: Harcourt, Brace & Co., 1934. pp. xi + 495. $4.50.

With this book Mr. Mumford adds to his writings in the field of social interpretation a work that is both historical and prophet. It is a study of the cultural effects of the development of "the machine," defined as "the entire technological complex."

Before he describes the future position in society, which it is his hope that "the machine" will come to occupy, Mr. Mumford traces those "cultural preparations" and "agents of mechanization" that have brought "the machine" to its present place in our civilization concludes that there is nothing inevitable in the relationship that has existed between capitalism and "the machine." In the recognized evils of nineteenth- and twentieth-century society the latter, he says, has been essentially a "neutral agent." Capitalism has been the malicious element in the unnecessary partnership. Thus, it is possible for Mr. Mumford, as it has not been possible for so many other idealists, to build his Utopia about a firm acceptance of "the machine." He foresees a society in which this "neutral agent" is allied with and made to serve a new scale of social values organized around "human efficiency," instead of the old values dependent on pecuniary efficiency.

The history of "the machine" in its cultural setting is described in terms of two culture-epochs. The Eotechnic, extending from the thirteenth century to the end of the seventeenth, was the period of "organic resources" (wind, water, and wood) whose "goal" was "a greater intensification of life." The Paleotechnic, covering the eighteenth and nineteenth centuries, was an age of the supremacy of "inorganic" resources (coal, iron, and steel) and activity (mining, industrial "giantism," cultural murkiness, and hypocrisy). The "goal" of this period was a "quantification of life" and a shift from "life-values to pecuniary values"; this sets the stage for the economics of free enterprise – "The Empire of Muddle."

In elaborating his discussion of these eras, Mr Mumford draws generous inspiration from Sombart, Max Weber, Veblen, Patrick Geddes, Spengler, and even D. H. Lawrence. But, far from facing the methodological and intellectual problems involved in an "institutional" or "historical approach, Mr Mumford intensifies them. His complete, unquestioning subjectivism has at times the quality of lyric poetry rather than sociological interpretation. The reader cannot but be suspicious of an eclecticism of this sort, which reveals, in addition, an almost total dependence on secondary historical sources.

It is, however, in Mr Mumford's description of the Neotechnic era, a possible, and for him desirable, future culture period, that he is open to most severe criticism. This is to be the era of a return to "organic" resources (water, electricity, aluminum, and the precious alloys) and activity (regionalism, small units, "functionalism" in art and life). The "goal" will be complete automatism of production ("displacement of the human proletariat") and a social assimilation of "the machine" culminating in "aesthetic efficiency." Unlike the other periods, this one is to be inaugurated by, and to exist upon, a basis of "social energetic." That is to say, he proposes a deliberate planning of every minimum aspect of culture in the interests of one value, "human efficiency." This planning will be comprehensive in scope, directing every phase of agriculture and industry, governing the growth and distribution of population, and "normalizing consumption." Finally, "creation is to be socialized"!

Surely Mr Mumford is the most sanguine of the "planners." He surpasses even Stuart Chase and the technocrats, from whom he borrows his concepts of an "economy of abundance" and of energy as ultimate value. We are told that the task of planning will be complicated (!) and that it will require the services of the geographer, the regional planner, the psychologist, the educator, the sociologist, and the skilled political administrator. Not a paragraph, however, is devoted to the economic, political, social, philosophical, educational, or geographic problems inherent in any program of State Planning.

Mr Mumford is to be congratulated on his attempt to provide consistent historical background for the humanistic idealism that is expressed in his Utopia. Nevertheless, there is uncertainty, to say the least, in his use of words vital to his meaning ("organic," "efficiency," "functional," etc.), and there is a lack of critical analysis and judgment in all the specifically economic discussion. One can only envy the confidence that Mr Mumford displays in his cavalier treatment of certain fundamental problems about which the last word has not been, and perhaps cannot be, said.

F. Taylor Ostrander
Williams College

ACKNOWLEDGMENTS

The correspondence between Walter Smith and Frank H. Knight is published with the permission of the University of Chicago Library. This correspondence was found in the Knight Papers by Ross B. Emmett who thoughtfully arranged for copies to be made available to me for publication. *F. Taylor Ostrander's Book Review of Lewis Mumford's Technics and Civilization* (New York: Harcourt, Brace & Co., 1934) was published in the *Journal of Political Economy*, vol. 43, no. 3 (June 1935), pp. 419–421. © 1935 by the University of Chicago Press. The review is published here with the purpose of facilitating reader access. The correspondence between F. Taylor Ostrander and Frank H. Knight is published with the permission of the University of Chicago Library. The Editor of this material and of the volume of *Research in the History of Economic Thought and Methodology* in which it appears is grateful to all who have given permission and cooperated in this venture. Ostrander thanks his daughter, Tryntje Shapli, Professor Emeritus of Dance, California State Long Beach, for her enormous help with this project.

Although tempted to comment on the treatment given institutional economics in the letters, I will call attention only to Stunkel (2006) that I am not in complete agreement with it as institutional economics and that Chicago economics is open to criticism similar to that made of institutionalism by Knight and Ostrander.

REFERENCES

Samuels, W. J. (2004). F. Taylor Ostrander: A brief biography. *Research in the History of Economic Thought and Methodology, 22B,* 167–172. Volume 22B also contains Ostrander's notes on Knight's course on the history of economic thought.

Samuels, W. J. (2006). Material from economics 1, taught by Walter B. Smith, Williams College, Fall 1929. *Research in the History of Economic Thought and Methodology, 24B,* 3–54.

Stunkel, K. R. (2006). Vital standard and life economy: The economic thought of Lewis Mumford. *Journal of Economic Issues, 40*(1), 113–133.

PART II

MAURICE BECK HEXTER'S NOTES FROM HARVARD UNIVERSITY, 1921–1922

Edited by Marianne Johnson and Warren J. Samuels

INTRODUCTION

The notes reproduced below were taken by a student, Maurice Beck Hexter, at Harvard University during the academic year 1921–1922. The notes are typewritten and handsomely bound, entitled:

ECONOMIC THEORY 11 AND 12
PROFESSORS TAUSSIG, YOUNG, CARVER
1921–1922

The notes are effectively divided into three parts. The first section contains notes from Taussig's economics theory course, EC 11. The second section contains supplemental notes from this course; the third section is comprised of notes from T.N. Carver's course on the distribution of wealth, EC 12.

The supplemental notes are something of a puzzle. According to the Official Register of Harvard University, Vol. XVII, December 20, 1921, No. 51, Frank William Taussig was the only instructor of record for Economic Theory (EC 11). The initial notes seem to confirm that what is reproduced here is solely Taussig's

Economic Theory by Taussig, Young, and Carver at Harvard
Research in the History of Economic Thought and Methodology, Volume 28-C, 11–190
Copyright © 2010 by Emerald Group Publishing Limited
All rights of reproduction in any form reserved
ISSN: 0743-4154/doi:10.1108/S0743-4154(2010)000028C003

teaching, with frequent mention of his views recorded (e.g., "Taussig says"). However, in the "Supplementary Notes," attributed to both Taussig and Allyn A. Young, frequent mention is made of Young's views. Whether these notes are from lecture, recitation, or are Hexter's personal notes is unknown.

Frank William Taussig and Economics 11

Taussig (1859–1940) was one of a handful of premier U.S. economists during the first third of the 20th century. Born in St. Louis, Taussig completed his education at Harvard University in economics, graduating in 1879, having studied under Charles Dunbar. While Harvard was an early leader in American graduate education in economics, Taussig's training bore little resemblance to what would be considered sufficient training today.

The evolution of economic education bears some discussion, as Taussig oversaw the development of a modern graduate program at Harvard University during his nearly 50 years on the faculty. Harvard had established the first chair in economics in Charles Dunbar in 1871. In 1876, the time of Taussig's studies, Harvard was one of only three institutions to offer more than one economics course – the other two being Middlebury and Yale. They and Harvard offered two courses, one at the beginning level and one at the advanced (Laughlin, 1892). And while the first graduate courses in economics began to appear in America during this period, graduate study largely involved one or two undergraduate courses and a couple of years of independent study (Parrish, 1967). Motivated students generally opted to study in Europe, particularly Germany. For example, Richard T. Ely earned his PhD in economics in 1879 in Heidelberg.

After graduating, Taussig immediately began teaching economics at Harvard; he achieved a professorship in 1892 and served as chair from 1885 to 1935, when he was replaced by Joseph Schumpeter. Taussig served as the editor of the *Quarterly Journal of Economics* from 1889 to 1890 and from 1896 to 1935, the president of the American Economic Association in 1904 and 1905, and the chairperson of the United States Tariff Commission from 1917 to 1919.

By 1921–1922, under Taussig's leadership, the graduate curriculum had expanded to include theory and applied courses, of which Economics 11 was a central theory course. Economics 11 and 12 formed half of the grouping "Economic Theory and Method," rounded out by "History and Literature of Economics to the Year 1848" and "Modern Schools of Economic Thought." The former course was taught by Charles J. Bullock during the 1921–1922 academic year and the latter was taught by Allyn A. Young. These courses were primarily for graduate students. The rest of the graduate study program was comprised of courses from three groupings: (1) Statistics, (2) Economic History (two courses, neither being taught in 1921–1922), and (3) Applied Economics, including courses in Public Finance (Bullock), the Economics of Agriculture (Carver), International Trade and Tariff Problems (Taussig), Problems of Labor (Ripley), Business Corporations (Davis), Business Combinations (Davis), Public Ownership (Lincoln), Public Regulation (Lincoln, not taught in 1921–1922), Commercial Crises (Persons), and Selected Monetary Problems (Young).

Taussig's course focused heavily on the classical economics of Ricardo and Mill, the neoclassical approach of Marshall, and the American contributions of Walker and George. He had little patience for the marginalists, a fact that comes out plainly in the notes reproduced here. "The revolutionary changes that took place in economic theory in the subsequent decade did not manifest themselves at Harvard in the 1920s. Classical economics was dominant and its adequacy as a basis for policy was hardly ever questioned" (Carlson, 1969, p. 102). Yet despite some sympathy for the view of "American Exceptionalism," Taussig devotes virtually no time to the work of American Institutionalists, with the exception of a brief discussion of Veblen's *Theory of the Leisure Class.* Taussig describes his course as "a series of exercises in the 'Grand Style.' Austrian School and American followers, Clark, Fetter, and Fisher belong to class of 'grand style.' But don't point the way to further progress. Two most promising leads: (1) statistical method and its adaption to economic science ... (2) social, behaviorist psychology."

Valdemar Carlson, a student of Taussig's in the 1920s, remembers that Economics 11 was known as Taussig's course. Taussig who had trained as a lawyer at Harvard

> ... utilized a teaching technique that combined something of both the procedures of a prosecuting attorney and those of the case system of instruction ... he would assign a limited amount of reading in the leading authors of the classical and American tradition, e.g., Ricardo, Cairnes, Mill, Marshall, Böhm-Bawerk, and then ply the members of the class with questions. ...

> Taussig's method forced a concentrated attention to a topic or problem that no lecturer in my classroom experience had ever been able to evoke. ... Unlike a courtroom where the cross-examining lawyer can only call on the witness who has been sworn in, no student could relax because he might be called upon to reason his way through some theoretical problem. ...

> Taussig's teaching had a dramatic quality that elicited my admiration. He had been teaching classical economics for over a quarter of a century, and it was unlikely that any student would say anything about the theories of Ricardo, Mill, or Marshall that he had not heard many

times before. Yet each statement of the student was accepted enthusiastically as a fresh and original idea, which gave the neophyte a sense of importance. That the student might later be trapped by Taussig's penetrating queries and thus disclose his limited knowledge of facts or a confusion in his logic further emphasized the technique of a superior teacher. (Carlson, 1969, p. 104)

This approach explains much of the format and content of the notes reproduced here. While there is some use of graphs, very little mathematics are used in exposition of the theories presented – even those of Marshall. Carlson notes that by his retirement in the 1930s, Taussig was beginning to feel that his lack of mathematical training limited his ability to effectively use modern economic techniques.

Through his position at Harvard – as teacher, chairperson, and editor for 40 years of the *Quarterly Journal of Economics* – he had a profound influence on the course which economics was to take, though that course was somewhat narrower than his own. He specialized in international trade but was an eminent general economic theorist who also wrote on the psychology and sociology of economic life. For some people, notably Joseph A. Schumpeter, who Taussig brought to Harvard, he was the "American Marshall," ranking him with the eminent English economist, Alfred Marshall.

Allyn Abbot Young

Allyn Abbott Young (1876–1929) was one of the most highly regarded economic theorists of the early 20th century, notwithstanding the relative paucity of his publications. He achieved his reputation in part by a famous article on increasing returns and economic progress; in part through his teaching, including his role in the creation of at least two famous dissertations, those of Frank H. Knight and Edward H. Chamberlin; and in part through his contributions as co-author of several editions of Richard T. Ely's *Outlines of Economics*, then by far the leading college economics textbook in the United States.

An outstanding student, Young moved in and out of academics throughout his early life. He enrolled in graduate school at the University of Wisconsin in 1898 and studied under Ely. After a couple of years at the U.S. Census, Young returned to Wisconsin as an economics instructor in 1901; he completed his PhD there in 1902. He taught at Western Reserve, Dartmouth, and Wisconsin before becoming the head of the economics department at Stanford. He spent the 1910–1911 year visiting at Harvard before moving on to Washington University in St. Louis, Cornell, and the Bureau of Statistical Research in Washington, DC. He accepted a position at Harvard in 1920, where he remained until 1927, when he moved to the London School of Economics. "Young never wished to stay for any length of time in any one university. He believed that the process of adjusting himself to new educational policies and colleagues would stimulate his imagination and broaden his knowledge" (Carlson, 1969, p. 106).

Regarding Young's courses at Harvard, which he attended in 1922–1923, Nobel Laureate Bertil Ohlin stated:

> I am inclined to believe that he was a man, who knew and thoroughly understood his subject – economics – better than anyone else I have met. I tested him by means of a question about the "Wicksell effect", i.e. the special aspects of the marginal productivity of capital, which at that time was practically unknown in most countries outside of Scandinavia. He immediately gave a fine account in a five minutes speech before the students. What characterizes Allyn Young as an economist was that he had deep understanding of all fields of economic theory while other economists knew well one third of the theory and had only superficial knowledge of the rest.

Carlson states that when enrolling at Harvard, he had never heard of Young. But,

> it was not long before I realized, however, that Young was the most highly respected economics professor at Harvard. ... His reputation as a scholar and a teacher was well deserved. He possessed in rare degree the quality of intellectual rigor combined with tolerance for new ideas. As a discussion leader, Young was the opposite pole from Taussig. Taussig tolerated no half-formulated ideas in his pedagogical pursuit of developing the student's logical thinking. Young took the least glimmer of insight or understanding expressed by a student and clothed it with an amazing amount of significance. (Carver, 1968, p. 107)

Thomas Nixon Carver and Economics 12

T.N. Carver (1865–1961) was born in Kirkville, Iowa, to Quaker parents. He studied at Iowa Wesleyan College, the University of Southern California, and Johns Hopkins before earning a PhD from Cornell University in 1894. At Johns Hopkins, Carver studied under John Bates Clark and Richard T. Ely. Carver came to Harvard in 1902 as a professor of political economy. He served as secretary-treasurer of the American Economics Association (1909–1913) and as president in 1916.

Carver was a socially conservative economist who worked in the tradition of J.B. Clark. He had little use for the theories of the American institutionalists, in particular Veblen, and was a ferverent antisocialist. Carver was heavily invested in deductive analysis for economics, though he would adopt statistics when he felt they would bolster his argument. His primary research and teaching interests centered on contemporary social problems, including issues in agriculture. Former students remembered that "whatever [the course's] title may have been, its purpose ... was to prove the inadequacies of socialism or any other alternative to capitalism" (Carlson, 1969, p. 109).

The notes reproduced here are from Economics 12, a half-year course entitled "The Distribution of Wealth," which was taught during the fall semester. Along with Economics 11, this course formed the core of economics theory courses for graduate students at Harvard.

Maurice Beck Hexter

The student Maurice Beck Hexter turned out to be quite eminent in his own right. He (June 30, 1891–October 28, 1990) was born in Cincinnati and received his BA from the University of Cincinnati in 1912, and the MA and PhD in social work/social ethics from Harvard in 1922 and 1924, respectively. At Harvard and Simmons College, he taught courses in social ethics; he was associated with the Department of Social Ethics at Harvard as instructor and tutor from 1921 to 1929. He worked in a series of positions in Jewish charitable organizations, starting in 1915: executive director of the Federation of Jewish Charities in Milwaukee, Cincinnati and Boston; administrator in Jerusalem of the Palestine Emergency Fund, 1929–1938, in which capacity he also served on several joint British–Palestinian committees; and high positions in the Federation of Jewish Philanthropies in New York, 1938–1967. He was active in founding schools of social work at Brandeis University, Hunter College, and Yeshiva University. He served on numerous panels overseeing the public welfare system of New York City. He received honorary degrees from some half dozen universities. He published a number of books, including *Social Consequences of Business Cycles* (Houghton Mifflin, 1925) and *Juvenile Employment and Labor Mobility in the Business Cycle* (Boston Child Labor Committee, 1927).

The Notes

For those interested in studying the evolution of Taussig's work, these notes provide invaluable insights into his thinking on economic methodology and social policy. The notes, typewritten and handsomely bound, have been in the possession of Warren Samuels for many years. Alas, so many years that he has forgotten how he acquired them. He thinks that he either found the bound notes in a used-book shop and purchased them, or was given the notes by Robert Lee Hale.

Very minimal stylistic changes or other corrections have been made to the notes. Articles were added for easier reading and many abbreviated words are now spelled out. In some cases, materials or notes in the margin are included in square brackets. In addition, occasional explanations or comments by the editors are also included in square brackets. All underlined phrases or words and all words written entirely in capital letters are reproduced exactly as they are written in the notes. Footnotes have been added for the aid of the reader.

We are indebted to Margaret Henderson and Subash Shrestha for scanning and initially correcting these materials.

References

Carlson, V. (1969). The education of an economist before the great depression. *American Journal of Economics and Sociology, 27*(1), 101–112.

Laughlin, J. L. (1892). The study of political economy in the United States. *Journal of Political Economy, 1*(1), 1–19 and Appendix pp. 143–151.

Parrish, J. (1967). Rise of economics as an academic discipline: The formative years to 1900. *Southern Economic Journal, 34*(1), 1–16.

F.W. TAUSSIG'S COURSE IN ECONOMIC THEORY

ECONOMIC THEORY 11
PROFESSOR TAUSSIG
1921–1922

MAURICE B. HEXTER

ECONOMICS 11

Sept. 29

Assignment

H. George – Progress and Poverty, Bk. I, Ch. I, II, IV.
F.A. Walker – The Wages Question, Ch. VIII, IX.

Oct. 4

Assignment

J.S. Mill, Bk. II, Ch. XI, SS. 21.

Discussion of Henry George's Progress & Poverty, Pub. 1880

With Frances Walker, marked break from old tradition. Associated with single tax. George a Cal. newspaperman saw growth of San Francisco, resultant poverty, and thus developed his theory. All his political economy based on John Stuart Mill, who was regarded then as classic storehouse and authority, and it required courage for George to take issue with him.

Part we are concerned with does not deal with single tax, but with economic theory.

George's Argument

1. In primitive society people live from hand to mouth – there is no capital. Wages then the product of labor. (Wages are reward for labor, or human exertion – Def.)
2. Society in its most highly elaborated form is same as fundamentally primitive society and governed by the same principles. Phenomena of primitive society gave clue to those of existing society.

3. Under complex division of labor no one produces anything in its entirety. At a given time, the body of laborers is producing what the body of laborers is simultaneously consuming. ... Current labor is supported by current production. [In margin: See Ch. III.]

George's Definition of Capital

Wealth not yet advanced to point where it can be consumed. Producer's capital. Orthodox idea. Goods in stock are still producer's goods, though in a sense finished.

George maintains there is no advance of capital.

Walker's Theory

Wages are the product of labor but under some circumstances wages are advanced from capital. Ex. Agricultural industries. Extent of advance depends on character of industry and financial development of country. But in ALL cases, advance or no, wages are paid out of labor, and amount of wages determined by product of labor, not by capital.

In farming on shares, the landlord gets ½ and negro ½ gets and during season landlord makes advances to negro.

Doctrinal implication of Walker

The fundamental process in wages is that wages are paid out of the product of labor. Sometimes advances of wages are made.

Oct. 8

Taussig – Wages & Capital, Ch. 6, 7, 9, 11.
Cairnes – Leading Principles, Part II, Ch. I.

Walker says that SS. 4–6 and 8–10, the wages-fund theory, closely connected with economic conditions following Napoleonic War.

Taussig disputes this theory and the above assignment gives the history which formed background of wage-fund theory. Was closely connected with disappearance of yeoman at end of 18th century and beginning of 19th century, and the organization of agriculture attendant upon this disappearance – enclosures, etc.

Walker's Wage-Fund Argument and Attitude of Classical School of Economists

Walker says that employers purchase labor for profit, and product determines the amount of wage.

Mill would grant that employer's motive in hiring labor is production, not because he has a fund which he must disburse. But Mill would say that wages do depend on the product of current industry; but the product of current industry is dependent on capital. Walker says capital does not affect wages only as it affects production; Mill the dependence of wages on capital is direct, not via production. Walker says equipment and character of labor determine product.

Walker's theory of origin of wages fund in Napoleonic Wars and their effects is [blank space]. Origin is in disappearance of yeoman.

Other Disputable Points

1. To what extent is there an advance?
   There are cases where there is no advance – cash-and-carry stores, street railway employees, etc.
   There are cases where there is partial advance, as in agricultural industry in West.
2. Importance and effect of character of laborer in determining product.
   Mill would claim that Walker's argument that given machinery, raw materials, and year's subsistence, that Englishmen would receive higher wage than East Indians because of greater efficiency – Mill would claim there would be no difference the first year, but that the efficiency of Englishmen would increase capital that the wage fund would be increased and [therefore] wages provided number of laborers remain the same.

Oct. 13

Walker's example of Englishman and East Indian, in which he claimed that given year's subsistence is guaranteed that Englishmen would get more because of greater efficiency. Walker ignores the machinery of exchange – tries to argue from simple case to complex.

George's example of the pyramid builders in Nile valley, who, as they work, are fed on products of Nile produced contemporaneously. Wage-fund supporter would say that both the men raising crops and the pyramid builders are fed on last year's crop – and so there is a continuous overlapping of product.

In both Walker's case and George's case food consumed not produced by contemporaneous labor.

Ex. 1. Butter – which includes labor of man who raised grain to feed cow.

Ex. 2. Tailor-made clothes – cloth made over long period of time.

When speaking of contemporaneous labor, remember everything takes time to produce. Consider things required in production of commodity. Finishing touches only put on by contemporaneous labor.

Cairnes' Approach to Wages-Fund Theory.

Thornton, a great friend of Mill's, and he opposed Mill's theory. Wrote book on "Labor; Its Rightful Claim and Wrongful Remedy." Attacked wage fund on basis of law of demand and supply. Mill wrote review of book and surrendered easily to Thornton. Mill not really very much interested in question. Interested in trade union socials, phase which really has no direct bearing in wage-fund theory.

Then came Cairnes, the last of the English Classical School – first Smith, Ricardo, Mills, then Cairnes.

Cairnes analyzes capital into:

1. Fixed capital
2. Raw material
3. Wages fund

In country like England, fixed capital predominant.

In U.S. as transformation into [blank in original] country means increase of amount of fixed capital and less for wages fund. Nature of country determines proportion of three parts.

Cairnes doesn't turn all of capital over to laborer – only part, and then only a transforming of one part to another part.

Cairnes refutes Laye's [possibly means Walter Layton] theory that the demand for commodities determines the demand for labor, and bases wage-fund theory on law of supply and demand.

Cairnes' method very different from Walker's. Walker's island with Englishmen and East Indians assumes a physically limited case. There are two possible kinds of limitations:

1. Physical limitations – food, clothes, etc.
2. Limitations of money

When we begin to think in terms of exchange and money, then an entirely different situation arises.

Cairnes thinks of capital as immediately controlled by person hiring laborer – money in hands of businessman to be expended as he determines.

Walker and George have different idea of capital – a physical quantity in hand, e.g., food, etc. – physically limited quantity.

Is Demand for Labor Predetermined?

Three factors in demand:

1. Character of individual
2. Possibility of profits
3. Funds available

Attitude of individual capitalists that wages fund be determined based on

a. Possibility of profits
b. Funds available

If capitalist is making good money, will put in more.

Therefore, this factor #1, the character of individual, is a very slow-acting force in the determination of wages fund.

Cairnes' wage-fund doctrine is that there is a minimum return to capital, and capital tends to reach that minimum return – a very dubious and disputable doctrine. In re-vamping wage-fund doctrine, Cairnes virtually gave up the doctrine.

Assignment

Taussig – Wages and Capital, Ch. I.

F.A. Walker – Business Profits.

Discussions I, p. 369

Pol. Econ., Part IV, Ch. IV.

Oct. 15

Persistent Cause of Confusion in Confusion between Money Wages and Wages.

Walker is referring to wages of East Indians and Englishmen, and George also, meant commodity wages, which are in stores, houses, etc. Thus wages not in hands of employer.

Ricardo, Mill and others thought of wages in hands of employer – impossible for real wages.

Money Wages.

Give up notion of money wages, and wares in hands of employer, and you raise numerous difficulties. Amount of money at disposal of employer may be very flexible. Thus raises question of barking, credit, exchange, etc. Funds available for investment accrue through savings of individuals. Theory of possibilities of promotion through mere banking inflation. (Huyhton's [no record found of Huyton] theory, University of Chicago.)

No reason for saying fixed fund of any sort.

Question of source of rest wages.

Year after year, same men doing same thing.

1910	A B C D E
1911	A B C D E
1912	A B C D E E – consumable commodities
1913	A B C D E
1914	A B C D E

Question – who produces 1914s E?

Walker and George say 1914s A B C D.
Taussig says 1910 A, 1911 B, 1912 C, 1913 D.

Preponderant part of labor performed in past.

Distinction between

1. Current product of labor
2. Product of current labor

$$1 = 1914 \quad E$$
$$2 = 1914 \quad A B C D$$

This distinction all-important in question at hand.

Last step in production ordinarily distribution in retail trade. Length of time involved indicated by rate of turnover of retail trade. Great variety – given 6 or 8 is his turnover – clothier has turnover of 3.

Walker wrong in saying labor paid out of current product. Current labor puts on finishing touches to product.

If this is admitted, there is no fund, but a <u>flow</u> real wages. Like reservoir, rate at which it flows out depends on rate at which it is fed to us.

Can it be called a <u>wages</u> flow?

> Taussig says there is no wages flow nor wages fund – but what Walker <u>calls national dividend</u>, not predetermined to certain uses. No absolutely fixed wages flow, though there is national dividend flow.

Is the discussion worthwhile?

Very important – relates to capital, saving, private property, and socialism. Connects with organization, creation, and management of capital. Walker and George didn't realize this connection of wage fund and theory of capital. By their theories, principles of capital and interest would go by the board. Walker staunch supporter of capitalism.

> Wage-fund doctrine has passed altogether.
> Böhm-Bawerk stresses time, using process of present production methods.
> Adam Smith's theory of capital, new creation by him.
> Walker confusion one of terms – inconsistency – not so great as George's.

Increase of real wages has to wait for increase in production, therefore over period of time – real advance of labor.

<u>Efficiency</u> means spirit of individual labor.

> Ex. Walker's comparison of Englishman and East Indian.

<u>Effectiveness</u> means outcome of block of labor involving all component parts – organization, management, tools, materials.

> A more important factor than mere efficiency.

Labor can get bigger share by organization; share is exaggerated.

Oct. 18

> <u>Walker</u> – Discussion, I. 383.
> MacVane[1] – *QJE*, Vol. II, 1, 453 [Business profits and wages: A rejoinder. *Quarterly Journal of Economics, 4* (2), 453–468]

<u>Question whether Incoming Flow of Real Income Could Be Quickly Increased.</u>

> Factors that would increase commodity income.
> Would change in attitude of laborers make great difference?

Taussig claims source of far-reaching advance must come from technical advance and improvement in organization. Ex. Discovery of electricity.

Industrial democracy has significance economically; but will not bring far-reaching change and improvement – Slow change in laborers themselves.

Walker's Theory of Distribution.

Walker stirred by Sedgwick's criticism that Walker had knocked down wage-fund doctrine without putting anything in its place.

Walker says:

1. Rent does not enter into cost of product. ("Ricardian of the Ricardians") by interest does enter into it.
2. There is no-rent land, but there is <u>not</u> no-interest capital.

<u>Wages</u> from the product of current industry – a residuum, not dependent on profits.

New Ideas of Walker.

1. Business profits a separate constituent in distribution – separate from interest. A fourth factor in problem of distribution – heretofore only

   1. Rent
   2. Interest
   3. Wages

2. Walker couples this in with theory of wages, which are

   1. Paid out of product of current industry.
   2. A residuum after rent, business profits and interest are paid.

An optimistic theory – hopeful attitude for laborers, and especially trade union movement.

Do the two theories $\left\{ \begin{array}{l} \text{Wages pd. out of present product.} \\ \\ \text{Business profits detrained as rent formula.} \end{array} \right.$

stand or fall together?
Not in conflict.

Walker's theory of payment of labor out of current industry doesn't involve theory of residual theory of wages, for Walker is viewing industry in the <u>long run</u>.

At a given time, business profits the residuum but in long run Walker says wages a residuum. Therefore, theory of business profits, wages from current product and residual theory must stand or fall together.

Walker's Theory of Profits.

Just as rent is due to difference in productiveness of two sites, so business profits is the entrepreneur's share of product of industry, amount due to superior ability or opportunities of employee.

A rent of land is due to

1. Inherent advantages (fertility, etc.)
2. Advantages of location

In business, profits due to greater productivity due to

1. Superior ability
2. Superior opportunity

Walker says ability the greater factor, minimizing importance of the advance.

Distinction Between Profits and Wages.

No-profits employer is the employer who is producing at the marginal cost of production.

Oct. 20.

Nature of Margin of Cultivation.

With regard to business profits, analogous to Ricardian theory of rent. Commodities sell at point where there is no rent, defined in terms of rent.
    Margin of cultivation with regard to profit is the no-profit stage.
    F.B. Hawley deduces risk theory of profit-margin of return to employer is remuneration for risk.
    Walker would say Vail, getting $100,000 a year salary from Tel. Co. is getting commuted profits, i.e., amount which he could get if in business for himself – salary and snare in business included in $100,000.
    Walker doesn't mean what Hawley means in his risk theory. Walker's theory presumes a more established, generally distributed of salaried wage men.
    No-profits employer according to Walker is man who can't make a success of conduct of business by himself and accepts employment by others – cashier,

superintendent, overseer; a barely decent living according to middle class standards. Ten years ago would have got $1,500. Today $3,000 salary. This man working for himself is no-profit man and his returns at the margin of cultivation are called wages.

No-profits man is

1. poorest man who stays in business;
2. receives remuneration which is no-profits – remuneration which is about that he would get if working for someone else.

No-profits might under Walker's; reasoning be thought of as "necessary profits."
    Wages are what is left when profit, rent, interest are taken out.
    Profits are the entrepreneur's share of product of industry over and above the cost of production to the marginal producer, i.e., man who produces at greatest disadvantage.

Oct. 22

Assignment

Ricardo – "Prin. Pol. Econ.", Ch. 1

Explanation of Walker's General Attitude.

Was at time of [blank space in original] president of M.I.T. Before had been Professor at Yale and head of U.S. Census.
    Trustees of the M.I.T. made up of Boston businessmen – especially, true of Executive Committee. Probably contact with such men influenced writing and concept of profits accruing from able administration of affairs.
    From this point of view we wish to discuss his reasoning. Walker's view too optimistic, too comforting.

Is Walker Reasoning in a Circle?

By analyzing Walker's concept, the no-profits man makes wages – man above no-profits employee gets composite income:

1. Wages (compensation to marginal producer)
2. Profits (differential accruing through superior ability)

Walker says wages based on anticipated value of product – advance based not on capital, but anticipated value of product.

Walker says after rent, interest and profits are taken out, wages are residual; claim is that you can't determine profits until you know the wages, which enter into cost of production, so wages are no more residual than profits.

Walker says profits are due to special causes and not dependent on wages.

Suppose Walker admitted he was hazy in description of no-profits man – but meant head bookkeeper, superintendent, type class into which poorer quality of employees go for refuge – a prosperously situated, noncompeting group. On basis of this, he said he had in Reid a particular grade of wage and in residual theory meant general wages. Two types of wages:

1. Residual theory – <u>general rate</u>
2. Profits theory – <u>particular rate</u>

Characteristic Features of Walker's Theory of Distribution.

1. Application of theory of rent to profits   I
2. Residual product of product = wages

Is there an inconsistency here?

Some modern economists take reverse attitude – profits are residual, wages marginal.

Oct. 25

Assignment

<u>Adam Smith</u> – Bk. I, Ch. V, about 2/5.
<u>Mill</u> – Bk. III, Ch. XV.

Justification of General Residual Wage Theory.

An optimistic view and successor to optimistic laissez-faire view of McCullough, Perry. Walker constantly attacked this and wage-fund doctrine.

Walker substituted an equally optimistic view that increased benefits went to laboring class if they only demanded it.

This residual theory now practically gone – most people, if they have residual theory, make it applicable to business profits.

Walker's work not to be belittled; did much to stir up discussion and clarify ideas.

Ricardo's Theory of Value.

Value of Commodity.

> (is in proportion determined by the quality and amount of labor required to obtain it.)
>
> Businessman thinks of cost of production cost in money terms.
>
> Ricardo's theory not the value of commodity in terms of cost of production. (Read Ricardo and see how little he uses the word, cost.)

Argument.

1. In early state of society, exchangeable value of commodities depends almost exclusively on comparative quantity of labor expended on each.

Cliff-Leslie – Essays on Political Economy.[2]

Contemporary of Laye [unidentifiable; maybe Walter Layton], Thornton, Cairnes. Well-known dissident.

Minor premise of Ricardo, he says is that exchange value of commodities in early societies determined by amount of labor.

Major premise that early days and commercial community of today governed by same principles.

Leslie claims minor premise untrue – the urgency of demand the determining factor, things done haphazard. Ricardo would have met objection by saying that he doesn't know savages, but really it makes little difference. But he thinks that workmen got pretty much fair return for the labor expended, and in the main this holds in modern times.

Ricardo goes on by saying no commodity can be a standard of value, since it fluctuates. Also, money is very uncertain standard of value. Concludes that labor is an invariable standard of value.

Adam Smith says labor and corn exchange for each other in same relation throughout years – so corn he takes as the invariable measure of value, and measures value of labor in terms of corn – more convenient commodity than labor. Ricardo supposes the quantity of corn given in return for a quantity of labor varies.

Smith's two theories.

1. Commodities exchange for each other in proportion to labor determined first price (i.e., quantity of labor involved).
2. The quantity of commodities that labor would exchange for would determine first price.

That is, quantity of labor it will exchange for:
1. Original purchase price = labor bestowed.
2. Original purchase price = Amount of labor commodity will exchange for.

Ricardo claims Adam Smith dealing with two different principles which he tries to merge into one. Says Smith's attempt to secure a permanent standard of value is impossible, but he says relative value of commodities at any one time can be determined by quantity of labor expended.

Value is a problem of relation at any given time.

Oct. 27

Are not George and Ricardo alike in this method development of theory on basis of assumption that the principles which underlying primitive society are the same as those in complex society, i.e., deductive method.

Ch. 1, Sec. 2.

Ricardo says that labor of different qualities differently rewarded, but this causes no variation in relative value of commodities. Subject of controversy between Ricardo and [blank in original].

Adam Smith had said about all there was to say on differences in wages, and Ricardo swallowed his theory whole. A.S. says differences of wages were of equalizing sort – higher paid wages were in return for strenuousness, greater skill, larger preparations, etc. This assumes all men are created par and equal – disregards inherent differences in men.

Ricardo accepted this and didn't bother about it. To us social stratification is off great interest because we are more alive to causes of inequalities and means of removal. Ricardo not interested in social causes – interested in mechanism of economics. This is reason for the way Ricardo passes over subject.

Ricardo says, assuming scale to be fixed, and thereafter changes in value must be due to quantity of labor. (Sec. 2, Ch. I.)

Section III.

Not only labor applied immediately to commodities affects their value, but labor bestowed on implements, tools, building.

(NOTE 1) Here the genesis of proposition in Ricardo and economists thereafter, that all the operations of the capitalists are resolvable in a succession of advances to the laborer.

Mill follows Ricardo in this – whole capitalistic process is nothing more than this.

> (NOTE 2) This theory raises question of Profits. Ricardo says sale of commodity registers value, and in determining price.

Ricardo considers everything under system of free competition; and profits are the same everywhere at a given time; therefore, since they are the same, the same proportion goes to profits, and prices, made up of profits and quantity of labor bestowed – exchange value is determined by quantity of labor bestowed. Fundamental determining cause is quantity of labor.

Laborers	Yearly Earnings	Advances of Capital
100	£50	£5000
	10% profits – 500	£5500 selling price
	9% profits – 400	£5400 selling price
		Not right

Machine Laborers	Earnings	Advances
100	£50	£5000
	10% – 500	5500 selling price

N.B. Change in profits involving fall does not affect value as wages would go up, i.e., profits high or low exactly in proportion as wages are low or high.

Cloth 100   £50   £5000   (can't sell for £5500 for machine
                                   = Labor which has to be recompensed).

       Profit 10%   <u>500</u>

Therefore, 10% profit on machine = 5500
                                     <u>550</u>
                                    6050

When Ricardo says part of labor of smith, carpenter, etc. who helped to build building and equipment must be included in value, i.e., analogous to amortization.

Ricardo assumes that implements are durable, no wear and tear. Significant in indicating Ricardo's awkwardness in reasoning.

Suppose in above that profits go down to 9%.

Cloth 100 @ 50½	=	5050	Labor
Profits @ 9%		<u>450</u>	Profits
		5500	

Profits on machine @ 9%	<u>495</u>	Profits on machine
	5995	

Difference due to proportion in division of proceeds between labor and capitalist. Therefore, independent division of proceeds between labor and capital causes change in value. Thus, simply a modification of original theory.

Change due to introduction of fixed capital in manufacture of cloth.

That is, the subsidiary modification of theory is that employment of machinery and other fixed and durable capital modifies principle that quantity of labor regulates value.

Ricardo assumes prices constant and value of money remains the same.

Oct. 29

Assignment

Mill – Bk. IV, Ch. III, SS. 4

Significance of Ricardo's Quantification as Theory of Value.

Theory of Value.

States that this modification that employment of machinery and other durable capital affects value is comparatively slight in its effects – not so with variation of value in proportion to quantity of labor involved.

Now we would lay emphasis on profits. How great in Ricardo's reasoning was place of profits.

If we asked Ricardo why he laid such emphasis, he would be puzzled. Ricardo had ironclad consistence of reasoning. Adam Smith more inconsistent. Ricardo was consistent, exact, accurate in reasoning. Worked with figures, an intellectual plaything to him. Not merely a mental exercise.

It is beginning of kind of reasoning in which British School excelled.

When Ricardo speaks of rise in wages, does not mean monetary phenomena, but phenomena of distribution proper. Assumes price remains the same and value of money stable likewise – and value of gold he thinks is determined by quantity of labor bestowed, and therefore, regards money as invariable standard of value – forgot later his hypothetical reasoning.

Ricardo introduced in political economy this kind of reasoning – differentiated between price phenomena and money phenomena. This method he established alone.

Ricardo on Rent.

Rent is that portion of the produce of the earth which is paid to the landlord for the use of the original and indestructible powers of soil.

Here not attempting definition of rent; but making distinction between rent of land and rent of mines. Say rent of mines if not yielded by indestructible Novices of soil. Rent due to scarcity of material within mine.

Rent of land different from rent for timber, which when gone is gone for good-and-all – not rent of virgin forest, but rent for land on which to grow forests.

Can it be said with regard to agricultural land that there are original and indestructible powers of soil for which rent is paid?

Ricardo's Theory of Rent.

Rent is always the difference between produce obtained by employment of two equal quantities of capital and labor.

Henry C. Carey (1830–1870) began as free-trader, upholder of classical school – because protectionist, greenbacker, sociologist. Wrote "Past, Present, and Future" (1840) in which he attacked Ricardo's rent theory – said men began with poor shallow soil and worked gradually toward best soils. Ex. U.S. settlers, i.e., more easily worked poorer soil, to heavier, more fertile soil.

Defenders would say that with poorer [blank in original] and implements he could perhaps work poorer land first.

Ricardo would say he knew nothing about it. If he looked into historical evidence he would have been forced to admit its force of argument.

In working from poorer to better land, poorer land after dropped out, therefore there would be no rent. Ex. Abandoned farms in N.E. [New England] as high land. Possible that with increase in population there will be a recession to poorer lands and then the differential arises as better lands in form of rent.

If all land were equally fertile and equally distant from market, would there be rent?

Von Thünen – *Der Isolieter Staat.*

Assumed city market in center of concentric circles, in which difference in fertility would be offset by difference in distance.

MARKET   Nearer land less fertile but more accessible.

Nov. 1

Ia

Capital	Product	Profit @ 16 $2/3$%	Rent
60	100	10	30
60	90	10	20
60	80	10	10
60	70	10	0
	340		60

Ib
@ 37.5%

Capital	Product		Rent
60	125	45	30
60	115	45	20
60	105	45	10
60	95	45	0
	440		60

Ic
@58 $2/3$%

Capital	Product		Rent
60	125	35	20
60	115	35	10
60	105	35	0
	345		30

IIa
@ 25%

Capital	Product		Rent
50	100	12 $1/2$	37 $1/2$
60	100	15	25
70	100	17 $1/2$	12 $1/2$
80	100	20	0

IIb
@ 33 $1/3$%

Capital	Product		Rent
50	100	15	40
60	100	18 $1/3$	26 $2/3$
70	100	21 $1/3$	13 $1/3$
80	100	25	0

IIc

17 $\frac{1}{2}$	100	15	37 $\frac{1}{8}$
56 $\frac{1}{4}$	100	18 $\frac{3}{4}$	25
65 $\frac{5}{8}$	100	21 $\frac{7}{8}$	12 $\frac{1}{2}$
75	100	25	0

Assumption of all land cultivated, all equally fertile, will there be rent?

Ricardo says immaterial whether you descend to use of poorer land or poorer uses of same land. Always land which returns only returns to capital and labor.

Ricardo doesn't suppose always a limit of no-rent land, but always a margin, with returns only to capital and labor.

Extensive vs. Intensive Cultivation.

American farmer knows production will cost him less if he uses more land. English farmer knows it is better to cultivate intensively. In England, practically all cultivated land, because all cultivated intensively to point of diminishing returns – fallacy to ascribe to Ricardo's theory that there must be no-rent land. Farmers in England cultivate more advantageously and therefore get larger differential.

American farmer cultivating wheat and getting 15 bushels to acre and could get 30 bushels. With increasing population, more intensive farming will come – but with it will come different agricultural methods, including rotation of crops, artificial fertilizer, etc. Change will come slowly – will mean new agricultural economy.

Von Thünen in his *Isolieter Staat* says degree of scientific farming must change slowly and change from one form of agricultural organization not easy:

--------------------- diminished agriculture

------------------ spade labor

--------------- general farming – grain crop

----------- pastoral occupation

Illustrations show that:

1. Way in which fundamental principles work out.
2. Necessity for modification of fundamental principles in application.

See Figures on Pages 15 and 16 [meaning previous pages]

Ia. Original returns of successive portions of capital
Ib. Suppose invention increasing produce

Ic. Ricardo assumes fixed demand for corn, therefore fall in price – grade 4 land will go out of cultivation, diminution in corn rent and diminution in money rent, because value of corn is lower.

IIa. Assumes fixed amount of product and variable amount of capital (in I assumes variable product and fixed capital).

Profits determined by return to capital at margin of cultivation.

Profits here vary because of varying amount of capital.

Difference then is <u>rent</u>, which varies.

IIb. No increase in amount of product, but invention allows less investment of capital. (comes from theory that capitalists' operations resolvable into succession of advances to laborers.)

Rent again the differential.

Ricardo says, under these circumstances there will be no alteration in corn rent: Wrong in this – figures show it.

He would have said he meant <u>proportion</u> remained the same. This is correct (IIIa).

Shows exactness of reasoning of Ricardo, which he tried to import into political economy.

Mill's difference which he worked out from basis of Ricardo's

Nov. 3. See Figures for Nov. 1.

Insignificant. What Ricardo meant was <u>proportional increase</u>.

Makes assumption of economic differences in rates of profits. Characteristic of Ricardo to bring out unprofitable cases to work out logic of the case. Doesn't care much about extreme suppositions to prove his point. Method of deductive school.

<u>Ricardo on Wages.</u>

Natural price of Labor (From A. Smith = concept of normal price.)

Application of theory of natural and market price of commodity to natural and market price of labor, drawing analogy.

<u>Market price</u> is price paid for it from natural operation of proportion of supply and demand.

In definition of <u>capital,</u> he includes

1. Food and clothing
2. Tools, raw materials, machinery – but thereafter (2) drops out and be considered as consisting of food and clothing. This neglect due to theory of operations of capitalists resolvable into succession of advances to laborers – and tools, machinery, etc. – new advances from previous capital; and Ricardo considers only present forms of food and clothing. Thus it [blank in original] and unconsciously supports wage-fund doctrine.

Relation of Market Price and Capital.

1. Capital may increase in quantity – in value at same time, under conditions diminishing returns.
   In this case, n price and m price will conform most speedily, and situation of laborer not much improved.
2. Capital may increase without increase in value, or even less value.
   Situation of laborer more improved.

In both cases, market price of labor will rise. [Question mark indicated in pencil in margin]

Relation of Natural Price of Wages and Capital.

Natural rate of wages is mere subsistence wage. LaSalle[3] uses this theory as Ricardo's. Was he right in ascribing this theory of ironclad law of wages to Ricardo?

Does definition of natural wage as enough to perpetuate race allow for flexibility in ironclad wage through theory of influence of increased standard of living?

Ricardo says in terms of corn, with increase of price of corn, money wages rise corn wages fall; and offset each other so enjoyments would be same. But as other commodities would go up in proportion as raw produce enters into competition, he would pay more for some of them – so in spite of increase in wages, condition of laborer would be worse.

Two interpretations of this qualification:

1. Apology for inaccuracy of statement at first
2. When price of grain goes up money wages rise but not enough to make him as well off as before.
   c.f. Ricardo on Value, p. 11.

In Ricardo, a number of passages which indicate disposition to believe that as food increases in price, money wages don't go up quite enough to offset it therefore laborer not as well off as before.

This indicates that Ricardo thought tendency of standard of living was to disintegrate (p. 57), "in advance of soviets, wages tend to fall, as far as regulated by supply and demand – for supply of laborers continue to increase at same rate, while demand is slower. [No end quotation mark in original.] Ricardo thought of standard of living determined natural rate of wages.

Thought standard of living fixed, of if anything with downward tendency.

Therefore, Ricardo rightly regarded as $\begin{cases} \text{progenitor} \\ \\ \text{expounder of Iron Law} \end{cases}$

Nov. 5

Assignment

Mill – Bk. 1, Ch. 10–12 [Labor on Increase of Production (Labor, Land, Capital)]

Ricardo on Profits.
    Definition of Profits

Ricardo meant gross profits, including in themselves interest.
   This the British traditional concept found in A. Smith. He regards interest of profits. Same concept held by Mill, Cairnes, and others up to time of Marshall. Ricardo regarded profits as same throughout industrial field. Mill differed here, but often came back to Ricardian treatment.
(Mill said profits include returns from

1. Interest
2. [Blank in original] -
3. Wages of nyt. – then forgets 2 and 3 and goes on to talk about #1 only.)

Thought "double-interest" = reasonable profits. Profits vary with interest – interest the indicator of profits.

Measure of profits. Profits depend on price of food.

"In all countries, at all times, profits depend on the quantity of labor requisite to provide necessaries for the laborers on that land or with that capital which yields no rent."

Consistency.

Is this consistent with Ricardian idea that actions of capitalists are resolvable in series of advances to laborers?

Profits depend on price of food, because standard of living is fixed therefore sets natural rate of wages.

Get suggestion that Ricardo quite get enough to maintain fixed standard of living – but in main standard of living is fixed.

Rise in wages does <u>not</u> mean rise in price.

Ricardo assumes value of money remains constant.

Rise in price of food means rise in wages, but <u>not</u> rise in price of commodities in general.

<u>Profits defend on price of food.</u>

Clings to this idea throughout.

An evidence of the effect of Malthus' teachings on the pressure of population. This doctrine permeated ec[onomics] throughout Great Britain in the 19th century.

Ricardo fell in line in this, but it fell in into Richard's bent for reasoning – his exact mathematical mind. Can reason thus that money wages depend on price of food.

Wages depend on price of food – as food goes up, wages go up, and profits fall.

How reconcile

1. the theory that profits depend on price of food, and
2. the theory that profits fall as wages rise, and vice versa.

Wages are high when laborer gets commodity produced into much labor. Fall in real wages due to the fact that corn is the product of less labor than before.

In other words, <u>profits defend on amount of labor necessary to produce the food which the laborer gets</u>.

See figures on pp. 66–68.

Farmer gets uniform return of £720 for his produce, produced by same amount of labor.

Quantity produced by that amount of labor varies, and as quantity decreases, wage increases, rent increases, and profits decrease.

p.72. Says all calculations have random basis, and merely for exemplification.

<u>Conclusion.</u>

Rate of profits tend to decline as society advances, though aggregate increases. (If profits decrease, and rate of wages increase, the result would be to decrease inequalities – this is theory of some economists.)

Would Ricardo accept this theory of decrease in inequalities? In Ricardo's theory of value based on quantity of labor bestowed, laborers would get a larger share, profits decline in rate though not in aggregate – finally increase in aggregate may fail to offset decline in rate. Ricardo assumes the increases in capital are the same – deceived by his mathematical reasoning. No reason to suppose equal increases.

Assignment

Mill – Bk. I, Ch. XIII, Bk. II, Ch. XI.

Nov. 8

Ricardo 1772–1823.

Writings:

1809	Letters on High Price of Bullion
1811	Reply to Bosanquet
1815	Essay on Influence of High Price of Corn
1816	Prop. for an Econ. and Secure Currency
1817	Principles (3rd ed. 1821)
1819–1825	In Parliament

I. Life of Ricardo. 1772–1823.

Jewish parentage. Rather orthodox Jew. Ricardo early left faith. Went into business at 20 and retired at 25 with a fortune. Ricardo broke away from Jewish faith and broke with father. Ricardo took advantage of fluctuations in securities. Retired and became landed proprietor on country estate.

Earliest interests in scientific subjects – geology and astronomy.

Became interested in political economy in 1799 when he read *Wealth of Nations*.

First appeared a writer in 1809 in writing on *High Price of Bullion*. McCulloch published one volume of collected works of David Ricardo after his death. In prefatory sketch, McCulloch says Ricardo's letters on price of bullion were begun without intention of publication – shows Ricardo's [blank in original] of lack of training. Finally, allowed writings to be published, and at once brought him a reputation. Thereafter published more readily but diffidently.

Reply to [Bernard] Bosanquet are beginnings of sound money doctrine – the quantity theory of money. Quantity theory didn't begin with him, but he clinched it. Depreciated paper currency find answer in these pamphlets of Ricardo.

1815 – Essay on Influence of High Price of Corn on Profits of Stock.

Extremely interesting. Tabular information. Contains compactly stated, all the doctrines of political economy. Brilliant and beautiful tables.

1816 – Proposals for Economic and Secure Currency.

Shows practicality of Ricardo. Very adaptable. This article basis of Act of Bank of England of 1834 on which Bank was eventually constructed. Also this article the germ of proposal of gold exchange standard of recent years, now applied in Philippines – currency redeemable in gold standard countries.

1817. Principles of Political Economy.

McCulloch's high appreciation of work.

1819–1823 – In Parliament.

At first unable to speak – later acquired considerable skill in debate – had a few supporters. A free trader, then regarded as a radical.

II. History of Ricardian Doctrines.

A. Theory of Value.

Two sources from Ricardo:

1. Adam Smith
2. [Blank in original]

Doctrine of price of corn as determining price of labor was the current doctrine circulated in 1817. But attached to that was corollary that price of food determining wages and wages in turn determining prices of commodities. Problems of money and distribution not kept apart. Malthus agreed that price of corn caused price of labor, and price of labor determined price of other commodities.

McCulloch held same theory.

Early in 1816, McCulloch published document on reduction of national debt in which he argued price of corn was going down therefore price of labor therefore price of other commodities. McCulloch recommended cutting rate of interest on national debt so that fund holders might not gain too much.

Ricardo didn't believe in this. Led to consideration of relation between corn wages and prices. Malthus never surrendered to Ricardo, but McCulloch and others did.

Letters.

Our knowledge of Ricardo enlarged by discovery of letters. Three sets of letters between

1. Malthus and Ricardo, discovered in 1887, edited by James Bonar
2. Ricardo and McCulloch, found by Professor Hollander in 1895
3. Ricardo and Crower, a stockbroker and fellow-friend of Ricardo. See also Hollander's *David Ricardo* (pub. 1910)

III. Ricardo's Relation to Contemporaries.

A. Malthus.

Ricardo convinced by Malthus's theory of population. On other subjects, Ricardo differed radically and represented exponent of opposite school. (Malthus and A. Smith were professors; Ricardo and John Stuart Mill were not.) Malthus' theory of value and distribution has come to be more current – normal value depended on cost of production at hands of capitalist employer – i.e. depends on wages, whereas Ricardo held, it depended on quantity of labor bestowed.

Ricardo's distribution theory – wages, profit, rent – established current views, but Malthus' theory of value the basis of current view.

Ricardo differed with Malthus about rent. Malthus maintained rent was sign of bounty of nature. Ricardo, it was the sign of niggardliness of nature. (Ricardo is better.) On social significance of rent, they differed; Malthus said rent made necessary leisure possible and as a reward to laudable exertion rent was just. Malthus uses Ricardo as example of desirability of rent for Ricardo was landed proprietor.

IV. Position of Ricardo.

In one sense, Ricardo's theory not important. Wages on corn, prices on wages, profits on corn, rent a differential – all this belongs to bygone ages. So far as theory of interest is concerned it has gone beyond point Ricardo never dreamed of.

As far as rent – as a differential – more of Ricardian doctrine remains, though much qualified.

As for theory of value, so many new problems involved that it has gone.

More remains of Ricardo's discussion of money and application of quantity theory. But even here base quantity theory has been tremendously modified and amplified so not very recognizable.

Theory of international trade remains more intact. Intellectually, Ricardo's theory – the substantive doctrines themselves – hold their own more than any other Ricardian doctrine.

Ricardo introduced into political economy a <u>new method</u>, a new consistency of reasoning, which is a permanent contribution to the subject. Tied rent, wages, etc. all together with theory of value and showed unity of subjects of economics as a whole.

Ricardo never got much of a hearing on the continent. Never has been on continent a consistency and unity of reasoning which has been characteristic of English political economy. A realism has characterized English political economy.

Nov. 10

<u>Assignment</u>

Mill – Bk. II, Ch. XI, Ch. XIII, Sec. 3, 4.
        Bk. IV, Ch. VII.

<u>Ricardo on Wages vs. Prices.</u>

See "But it may be said I was considering effect of wages on price" – p. 59.

   Says there must be rise in prices because of rise in stages.

Ricardo says argument worked out on supposition that there is no foreign exchange, and there is stable measure of value and range of prices.

   Can there be rise in all prices, if gold is foreign production?

   Gold, if foreign production, will cause fall of prices.

   To say that commodities rise because wages rise is a contradiction – means increased demand for gold therefore rise in gold – but if commodities rise, gold falls in value – contradiction. If commodities rise in value, gold wouldn't come into [blank in original] high commodities, but would go out. Therefore, rise in wages must cause rise in commodities whether home or foreign gold.

<u>John Stuart Mill.</u>

<u>Laws of Production.</u>

        No final limit to labor.
        No serious obstacle in capital.
        Land is the limiting factor in production.

<u>Are the Laws of Production of the Nature of "Physical Truths."</u>

Law of increase of capital that increase depends on the effective desire for accumulation which varies with

1. Difference in climate
2. Difference in race
3. Difference in occupation
4. Difference in institutions

Adam Smith says the desire to save comes with us from the womb and goes with us to the grave, i.e., it partakes of nature of physical truth.

A. Smith would have been behaviorist.

Sombart's *Der Bourgeois* (1913) – German economist, pupil of Schmoller, a social democrat.

In *Bourgeois* a continuation of discussion of capitalism. Discusses the roots of saving. Says state of mind desire to accumulate on part of bourgeois is an artificial convention, not a part of natural man – a peculiar psychological development. Rolling up of tradition of money – making from this conventionalized development. Not behaviorist.

Therefore, question whether laws of increase of wealth are of nature of physical truth goes back to [blank in original] psychology, etc. as well as to economic theory for the answer.

May be a distinction between

a. primary instinct of accumulation from production, and
b. derived instinct of accumulation from social distinction, power, etc.

Conditions under which population increase takes place involve many elements not of nature of physical truths – more of nature of moral and volitional doctrine.

These so-called laws of production are really laws of the indefinite increase of production.

Mill concludes the definite limit to increase = land.

Nov. 12

Assignment

Mill on Profits – Bk. II, Ch. 15.

                Bk. IV, Ch. 4–6.

                Cf. Bk. I, Ch. 13.

Get Marshall's *Prin. of Econ.* (any except 1st ed.)

See Taussig on Mill

Mill on Wages.

Mill's statement of wage-fund theory as proportion between capital and population – a bare statement – was due to the fact that the specter of Malthusianism overshadows his entire argument, and he was mainly interested in the way his theory of wage fund indicates the dangers of over-population.

In first book, the three laws of production, showing the limiting factor is land – population can increase indefinitely. Product from soil cannot increase anywhere nearly as fast as population.

In book II, argues from wages-fund theory to danger of Malthusianism. Not nearly as effective argument as book I.

Discussion of Relation of High Price of Food and Wages.

Both Ricardo and Mill use standard of living in strict sense of standard to which population will adjust itself.

Ricardo reasoned that corn laws would not do any good – repeal would mean decline in money wages, no change in real wages, and profits would rise.

Ricardo thought rate of profits the touchstone of prosperity. Repeal of corn laws therefore would mean higher profits, more food = greater population therefore wages stationery.

Mill thought corn laws would not benefit laborers because increase in proportion to cheapness of food. With cheaper food, wages would not fall at once, but not sufficient time elapsing before fall of wages to allow for increased standard of living.

Mill's suggested method for improvement.

Increased standard of living by

1. Education
2. Colonization
   a. [Blank in original]
   b. Home colonization

Future of Laboring Class.

1. Profit-sharing – association of
2. Cooperation – 1. Capitalists and Laborers
                            2. Association Laborers

This a plant of slow growth. Conflicting theories in Mill.

1. [Blank in original]
2. Wage-fund theory – Malthusianism
3. Social reform $\begin{cases} \text{colonization – quick} \\ \text{cooperation – slow} \\ \text{education – slow} \end{cases}$

Mill interested in English conditions – thought that realization of this uplift, outlined above, plus system of peasant proprietorship might solve the English problem.

Mill not consistent in his theories as above.

Rochdale movement was hope of radicals in the 1870s.[4] Cairnes last of this group.

Nov. 15

Mill on Profits.

1. Concept of Profits.

Includes interest, insurance, and wages of management. (Cf. Ricardo – interest plus return for risk, etc. Ricardo says nothing of return for ability.)

Cf. Walker – profits a differential – returns for ability. Uniformity in rate. Profits between trades but not individuals.

Ricardo – uniformity of rate of profits; also Mill, though he said there was tendency to equality between trades and men of equal ability in them – but not equality between individuals.

Walker's doctrine is of tendency of equality of profits between trades; also Mill's doctrine, i.e., in those elements which have nothing to do with personal equation.

But wages of superintendent vary with ability of entrepreneur.

Mill, like Ricardo, meant gross profits, but analyzes more carefully and considers wages of management – but allowing for difference in ability of entrepreneurs, profits tend to an equality.

Rate of Profit.

Rate of profit depends on proportional share of laborer in product. Profits depend on advances to labor.

"Cause of Profit is that laborer produces more than is required for his support."

Magnitude of produce – therefore, gross profits depend on

1. Productivity of laborer
2. Proportional share of laborer.
        Latter determines rate of profits.

Ricardo said profits fall as wages rise, and vice versa, i.e., Mill says not <u>wages</u> but <u>cost of labor</u> determines profits.

Cost of labor a function of three variables

1. Efficiency
2. Real wages
3. Cost of production of commodities constituting real reward of labor

Nov. 17

<u>Assignment</u>

<u>Mill</u> – Bk. III, Ch. IV. (omit p. 6).
<u>Cairnes</u> – Pt. I, Ch. III (pp. 1, 2, 5, 6, 7).
<u>Mill</u> – Bk. II, Ch. XIV.
cf. Ricardo – Ch. I, p. 2 or 3).

Program:

> Friday – Mill, Bk. 3, Ch. IV (Shows relation between Mill and Ricardo)
> Monday – Mill, Bk. 2, Ch. XIV, and Cairnes (compare)

<u>Mill's Statement of Things on Which Profits Depended</u>.

Ricardo says profits depend on price of food.

> Meant fixed, unchanging standard of living. Had Malthusian theory in mind.

Mill says profits depend in laborer getting more than necessary for his support.
    Not [blank in original] stating Ricardo's

<u>Profits – Diff. Statements in Mill</u>.

1. Cause of profits that laborer produces more than is necessary for his support.
2. Profit consists of the excess of the produce above the advances to labor.

3. Profits depend on the cost of labor.
4. "   " on excess over the cost of production. (See #2 above.)
5. Profits depend on amount of capital which is regulated by abstraction of capital through
   a. improvements
   b. emigration

[Numbering as in original notes]

2. <u>Profits consist of excess of produce above the advances to labor.</u>
   This Ricardo's theory.

3. <u>Profits depend on cost of labor.</u>
   Function of three variables:
   a. efficiency of labor
   b. amount of real wages – commodity wages
       Ricardo meant (b), real wages – value of wages in exchange
   c. Cost of production or procuring of commodities which constitute real reward to labor.

   When cost of production is greater, efficiency of labor less, and vice versa. Therefore (1) and (3) come to the same thing.

   (In Ricardo the one thing affecting efficiency of labor was the quality of land used.)

   This endeavor to more refined statement that profits due to fact that laborer produced more than was turned over to him.

   Therefore, this is not Ricardo's doctrine at all. Pretends to be Ricardo's statement but isn't.

   Therefore, Mill's is really an analysis of mechanism by which profits arise – not analysis of <u>cause</u> of profits.

<u>Tendency of Profits to a Minimum.</u>

Mill's law of accumulation of capital depends on effective desire to save. Concluded no obstacle to [blank in original] to production in capital.
   Minimum point of profits is that which is just enough to induce people to save.
   Depends therefore on effective desire for accumulation.
   In this chapter her means profits in the sense of interest, not concept of gross profits, including interest, insurance, wages of superintends – which he had in first chapter. Thus he falls back into old concept of profits – rate of interest.

Nothing said of effect on gross profits – wages of supt. and risk.

Inconsistent – here says profits depend on effective desire for accumulation. (Before said profits depend on cost of labor – here trading mechanism.)

Here really has a product theory of profits, more like Walker. Direct implication of such a theory in tendency of profits to a minimum at point where returns are just enough to promote same.

> Thus, a doctrine of stationary return to capital.
> (cf. Ricardo's pessimistic doctrine of stationary return to labor.)

Effect of Improvements in Production in Profits.

Ricardo's Analysis.

> An improvement in production of commodities consumed by laborers reduces money wages, leaves real wages intact, and increase Profits.

> An improvement in production of commodities consumed by rich it does not raise profits, capitalists are bettered in condition in enjoyments and possibly they may be induced to save more and might ultimately affect rate of profits.

> Ricardian analysis here – improvements affecting laborers leave real wages same – profits increase.

[In margin, "Gas engine theory"]

Mill's Analysis.

> Doctrine of successive explosions – each improvement soon exhausts itself. Accumulation follows fast on heels of improvements. When improvements come rapidly, rate of interest may be kept up for some time.

> In stationary state, interest may reach absolute minimum – not yet here because of improvements.

> Each improvement gives occasion for business profits.

> 1. Distinction between absolute and practical.
>   Practical minimum reached before absolute. Capital then flows abroad, determined by practical minimum. Practical minimum is higher in England.

Nov. 22

John Stuart Mill. 1806–1873

Scion of Ricardo

Father of Mill, James Mill, well-known writer – "Commerce Defended" shares with Jean Baptist the honor of doctrine impossibility of over-production.

1. Education of J.S. Mill
    See Autobiography (pub. 1870).

Remarkable education – history at 6; Latin at 8; 1810–1813 lived in London – walked with father, relative results of reading from 8 to 12 – Virgil, Ovid, Salust, Cicero, Greek drama, and philosophy; 12 – logic, philosophy, Greek, Latin.

Introduction to Political Economy.

Father got him complete course. Ricardo a close friend of father's – used his text. Papers written by father formed basis of his own *Principles*.
  On money, read Ricardo's pamphlets, followed by A. Smith, with companions.

2. Visit to France 1820–1821.
    Went to house of J.B. Say, the French expounder of A. Smith. Prom then on, gave more attention to continently affairs and discussions as well as to social questions – including socialism. Result of visit.

3. Influence of Meetings at home of Groat.

Became acquainted with writing of Bentham, Utilitarians – philosophical radicals, free-traders, liberals.
  Groat lent room in house for meeting for discussions of

1. Political economy
    [Began with discussion of James Mills' Pol. Econ. – thence Ricardo and Bailey on Value (Bailey a protester vs. Ricardo). Theory of international value emanated from these discussions.]

4. In 1823 (17 years) Examiner of Indian Correspondence in East India Co.

James Mill wrote *History of British India* (1818), read proofs and manuscripts.
  For 35 years worked with East India, went up to be in charge of Indian correspondence thence to examiner. East Indian Co. went out of existence in 1858.
  Will wrote during evenings after work then the days.

5. In 1839 – *Essays on Some Unsettled Questions of Pol. Econ.* (Pub. 1844).

    1. Problems of Pol. Econ.
    2. Distribution
    3. Minutiae of International Trade.

    Writing on international trade very good.

6. Logic.

Inductive – long drawn out.
    Success of book due to Mill's art of exposition.

7. *Principles of Pol. Econ.* 1846–1867– (pub. 1849).

Written more rapidly than any other. Two years – with six months taken out.

Very successful – three editions before 1852. Not merely abstract science, but branch of whole, social philosophy.

A great literary and quantitative performance. Required little thinking – ideas well crystallized before beginning to write. Same circumstances accounts for its defects – written so fast, that consistency was not paramount. A bringing together of what range of economists up to Mill had done.

A remarkable mosaic – many [blank in original] so well put together sections don't appear. Doesn't form organic whole. Ideas are amended, improved, and made Mill's own, yet core comes from someone else. Interesting to trace sources.

Chapter in book IV on "Progress of Society" in which Mill detailed Ricardo's ideas of two kinds improvements due to rent, and also Ricardo's "Essay on High Price of Corn" – Beautifully done.

8. Other influences in life.

    a. 1826–1827 a mental crisis, probably neurasthenia. Great depression and gloom. Led to change in his utilitarianism.

    Two results:
    1. Change in hedonistic utilitarianism.
    Happiness only to be attained indirect – have mind on happiness of others.
    2. Importance of poetry and art.
    Read Wordsworth, which satisfied him.

    b. Influences of Helen Taylor (1830–1858).

    Later married her.

    Wife controlled human element of his writings.

9. Nomination for Parliament in 1865.

Mill wrote little of importance after *Principles*.
Extraordinary circumstances. Time of parliamentary [blank in original]. Wrote open letter advocating woman suffrage – elected in spite of it – gave cause impetus.
   Mill unseated in Parliament in 1867.
   Mill's position in Parliament like Ricardo's. Like Ricardo, regarded with respect but thought a queer duck. Partly due to attitude on women's suffrage.
   Mill a strong advocate of proportional representation – wanted minority representation. Always an independent – supported his beliefs unflinchingly.

10. Summary

   Influence of Ricardo and Malthus.

   a. Ricardianism the background of Mill's *Political Economy*. Result of training by father. With Ricardo's influence went Malthus'.

   b. Humanism.

   A more cheerful strain as seen in chapter of future of laboring classes. Mill attributes it to his wife – more probably French influence.

   Reaction from extreme hedonism of Bentham.

   These two strains never
      1. Depressive
      2. Hopeful

In originality of thought, not equal to Ricardo or A. Smith; in influence it is widest. Remarkable achievement in bringing together diverse strains.

Nov. 24

Mill's Theory of Tendency of Profits to a Minimum.

Forces of Counteracting Tendency.

   1. Melting away of capital periodically in commercial crisis

      Nothing to this theory. Comprises money capital and industrial output of community, and it is working of real capital which counts. Mill thinking of capital in terms of money – can't [blank in original] away real capital. This confusion of money and real capital responsible for the theory.

      Where did this come from?

Consequences of Tendency to Minimum.

Corollary that overflow of capital from a country is not a loss. Ricardo said overflow <u>was</u> a loss.

In theory of international trade, question of overflow of capital a big problem. Advantage or not? Effect on distribution of wealth?

Mill says minimum return to point below which accumulation of capital will cease. According to this view, overflow of capital not disadvantageous.

Question hinges on whether there is a real or theoretical minimum below which accumulation will cease.

Cause of High Price of Glasses.

Monopoly = limitation of supply. It affects price insofar as it allows limitation of supply to be carried out.

Grinders of glasses have monopoly insofar as there is a limited number; but they don't control supply of grinders unless by some combination in which case they really exert monopoly.

High wages to grinders due to:

1. Disagreeableness, exactness of work

   Higher wages insofar as they call for long training are <u>cause</u> of high price.

   High wages insofar as they are due to limitation of supply are results of high price.

   Dentist requires long training and skill. If qualities are confined to small number of individuals, then high wages are results of high price.

   Necessary acquirement of skill a <u>cause</u> of high price.

Two influences on rate of return:

1. Labor necessary for acquiring skill
2. Limitation of numbers due to qualities necessary

Non-Competing Groups.

Horizontal division into groups according to degree of skill.

1. Unskilled laborers
2. Artisans
3. Highly skilled laborers – shopkeepers
4. Distinctly prosperous – lawyers, physicians, etc., big businessmen.

Cairnes.

1. Within non-competing groups, i.e., in free competition, value depends on quantity of labor – Ricardian theory. Difference in wages here due to difference in skill.
2. Between non-competing groups, restricted competition, value depends on reciprocal demand.

> Here prices high therefore get high wages.

> Wages the <u>result</u> of price.

General differences in level due to

1. Opportunity
2. Inborn ability – this an open question

Within non-competing group of skilled workers, wide difference in wages – for instance physician and college instructor – latter gets returns which make up for differences in money returns.

   Different degrees of attractiveness.

   Cairns doctrine of roughly separated non-competing groups sounds – value determined by reciprocal.

   Within each group differences regulated by Ricardian formula.

Nov. 26

Assignment

Marshall – Bk. III, Ch. II, III, VI.

Summary.

1. Terminology.

> <u>Cost</u>.

> Cairnes' (like Ricardo) = Quantity of labor – speaks of <u>sacrifice</u> of laborer, labor; of capitalist, abstinence labor and abstinence = cost.

> This sense of cost to be contrasted with everyday sense under capitalism of employer's outlay – from this point of view, cost is <u>wages</u>.

> This distinction is an old one. Goes back to Ricardo. Ricardo and Cairnes used <u>cost</u> in same sense.

> <u>Malthus</u> always claimed this a useless sense – he used it in terms of capitalist's outlay (= Cost).

This conflict of use, and with it real difference in opinions holds to our day.

Marshall in *Economics of Industry* said of phraseology later dropped, i.e., distinction between cost of production and expenses of production.

Founded on Cairnes' distinction between cost as used by Ricardo and Malthus and Mill in sacrifice, and cost in international trade.

Marshall meant cost = sacrifice and expenses in business sense.

So long as you have free competition between capitalists, expenses of production is the vital thing. Without free competition, division of booty between capital and labor unknown. Exchange within group – cost and production run together, i.e., free competition, expenses and cost conform to each other.

Tendency of Profits to Minimum.

Through Ricardo, Mill, Cairnes, find concept of uniform rate of return to capital. Mill and Cairnes think this level rate of profits is about a minimum which will content capital. Profits in accord with expenses of production, but only in free competition do cost and expenses conform to each other.

Marshall says Cairnes was not fair to Mill. Says Mill saw more of truth than Cairnes.
  Is this true?

Mill's Analysis of Causes of Differences in Wages.

Causes of differences taken almost directly from A. Smith.

1. Due to disagreeableness
2. Risk
3. Skill
4. Trust
5. Regularity of employment

These differences due to natural ability and difficult of acquiring skill and analyzed first by Mill. Two kinds of causes:

1. Causes which bring about restriction of competition:
   a. Differences in natural ability
   b. Differences due to difficulty of acquiring skill

Even with perfect freedom of competition, difference due to difficulty of acquiring skill.

2. Due to different degrees of disagreeableness.

Mill's statement of differences of wages covers the whole problem of nature vs. nurture, social; environment vs. heredity, etc.

Mill saw these differences and their significance as Cairnes didn't do.

Mill's Analysis of Cost of Production.

1. Quantity of labor the main factor.
2. General wages don't affect values (Ricardo).
3. Wages affect cost of production insofar as they vary between employments.
4. Profits affect value insofar as they are spread over time.

Cairnes' would say the between non-competing group's high wages not result of high prices, but both are affected by conditions of demand.

Mill had broader mind and saw more of truth than Cairnes; but Cairnes got more of mechanics of value than Mill and carried argument one step further.

Mill said particularly low gages in an occupation had an affect on value. He doesn't bring parts of his argument together to see that they bring together

Ricardo on Differences in Wages.

Says differences in wages are established, had no effect on value. Goes back directly to A. Smith.

Ricardo said there was no such thing as absolute standard of value – then speaks of absolute value. Perhaps thought of quantity of labor a sort of touchstone to absolute standard.

Scale of differences of wages is really subject to very slight changes over short periods. Differences due really to quantity of labor. Leads to question: why the differences in the beginning? Ricardo ignores question of social stratification – Mill didn't.

Conclusion.

Hierarchy of Theory of Differences in Wages

Ricardo's theory of quantity of labor.

Malthus' theory of cost of production.

Mill's mingling of two, theories – showed different social strata.

Cairnes' interaction of wages and value and systematic working out of principle of non-competing groups.

Nov. 29

Assignment

Wicksteed – Common Sense of P.L. – Bk. I, Ch. II.
                                    Bk. II, Ch. III
J.A. Hobson – Wealth & Welfare – Ch. XXII, Sec. I-8

Non-Competing Groups

- Prof. pays barber – takes relatively small part of money.
- Mechanic pays barber – on about equal terms.
- Prof. pays dentist – on about equal terms.

Same holds in international trade.

Within country, groups of unequal wealth exchange between each other, usually the principles involved are much more complicated – product requires sources from different groups. Brings in principle of value of one kind of source as compared with others. Complex demand – different kind of labor jointly contributing to satisfaction of a demand.

Marshall.

"Demand curve is always negatively inclined."
  Graphically illustrated, it slopes down to the right.
  Successive increases to quantity of commodity brings diminishing utility.

Assumes

1. No change in character of individual.
2. No intervening lapse of time.

       Art and music are the most real exceptions to principle.

       What demand curve is negatively inclined? Psychologist might question this.

"A Change of Demand."

An increase of demand when more of commodity is taken at same price, or same quantity at a higher price.

Graphically shown either by lifting curve or shifting to right.

Demand is quantity of commodity demanded.

> Cf. popular conception of more offered for commodity. When economists say that lowering price means increased demands is in popular market price.

Fisher: Two uses of "Demand"

1. Schedule sense
2. Market sense
   1. Schedule sense means that demand schedule has shifted – more of commodity taken at same price.
   2. Under conditions of market at given time, more of commodity will be taken at lower price.

      Therefore "Demand curve negatively inclined."

      Most commonly in subsequent discussion we mean demand in schedule sense.

Elasticity of Demand.

A question of degree – no such thing as inelastic demand.

B

B′   III Neutral Demand (Rectangular Hyperbolae)

B″

Demand curve such that whatever the quantity and price, the total amount spent remains the same. Therefore, elasticity of demand is unity.

Here change in price so that area $B = B' = B''$

I. Relatively inelastic demand   II. Relatively elastic demand

II. Elastic demand – where decrease in price means total amount spent increases (e.g., fresh vegetables)

III. Neutral demand – total amount spent remains equal (e.g., cotton) (statistics uncertain)

> Elasticity of demand for money is unity.

I. <u>Relatively inelastic demand</u> (other things =)

Drop or increase in price makes very little difference in quantity consumed.

(Elasticity sense
(<u>Third sense of increase in demand.</u>

<u>Elasticity</u> of demand is greater than unity. That is with drop of price, demand increased so that total amount spent is increased.

This a subdivision of <u>market sense</u>.

Ex. Drop in price of printing is increased demand for printing, that more compositors necessary.

<u>Dec. 1</u>

<u>An Extension of Value Theory.</u>

[In margin, Prof. Friday of Michigan][5]

I. [Blank in Original]

A. <u>Renaissance in Value Theory Imminent</u>

<u>Reasons for revival and sources</u>

1. Revival of price theory, in distributional sense.

Necessary to study causes of rise and fall in profits. Brought by steady rise in price.
2. Broader basis for value theory.
   a. Valuations for purpose of rate-making, amortization, taxation.
   b. Valuations in determining rights and justice.

Question arises in confiscation of property by the State. What is course of court in determining value in such cases. Many cases where majority stockholders merge corporations, etc., which involve question of market value to do justice to minority stockholders.

Question: Are all such cases ones of hypothetical price?

Hos, the, [sic] get exact nature of hypothetical market, and how work out just return in this hypothetical market.

B. Other cases involving valuation arising out of management.

Man in insurance company wishes some standard to compare with – see if actual and market value coincide.

Summary of   {Problems of public control,
types of   {Problems of administration and courts of justice equity,
value   {Problems arising out of management.

C. Courts and commissions today must have accurate basis for determining <u>reasonable rate</u> (for railroads, etc.) expressed in sum of money.

Involves careful pecuniary valuation.

Aim: To give sharp, definite criterion of value in terms of money – i.e., <u>pecuniary value</u>.

This pecuniary valuation performs same function as market value.

D. Summary.

In modern industrial society (1880 to present) with its new complexity, corporate management, and public control, a number of new institutions have function of making pecuniary valuation.

1. Market
2. Management
3. Public control of rate
4. Taxation
5. Courts
6. Majority stockholders

Each has developed literature, method of its own.

Economist remiss in leaving this field to lawyers, accountants, etc. Economist knows market value is relevant to remarket process. What is nature of value needs to be cleared up. No such thing as intrinsic worth. Only value public utility has is in evoking.

Friday – Value is quantitative expression embodying ideas of justice and equity.

Whole theory of private property is that regulation limits rights of private property.

Economist should show nature of value problem.

[In margin on left: Adequacy of valuation depends upon attainment of purpose you have in mind.]

Market regulates proportion between production and consumption, and we are letting it regulate distribution – and this last may result in unsatisfactory values.

II. <u>Revival of Interest and Price Theory Imminent.</u>

Renaissance of price theory will be due to fact that prices are related to same market process.

Economists will realize there are two kinds of market:

- competitive

- monopolistic

and that technique of market is essence of price-making problem. Take Taussig's method in dealing with tariff.

Results will be new grouping of markets.

A more numerous classification and more exact definition of causes which make for increasing, decreasing constant prices.

III. <u>Discussion</u>.

Valuation must be largely a question of policy. Public Service
Valuation depends on public policy.

Two-fold function of price $\begin{cases} \text{-Distributive} \\ \\ \text{-Competitive} \end{cases}$

1. Price which must be paid for use of labor, etc.
2. In competition, to eliminate less valuable forms by high rate of interest.

Dec. 3

<u>Depreciation: A Value Problem.</u>

Theory of value applied to depreciation as it arises in problems of railroads and rate-making.

Two theories.

Friday attacks theory that depreciation is an institution, not variable.

Two Schools of Opinion.

<u>Theoretical</u>

1. Allowance should be set up as depreciation reserve to last throughout life of plant.

   Rates should be made to cover depreciation charge.

Actual

2. Charges on depreciation due to abandonment. Regards theoretical depreciation as confiscation.

Both regard depreciation as value problem. Theoretical school makes only superficial study of problem of value. Determine value at a time by considering entire life of article and proportional decrease of value due to use through part of life.

Line of Argument of Actual School.

1. Decline in value is decline in pecuniary value.
2. Pecuniary value determined by market value.

    Actual school assumes continuous operation.

    J.E. Allison[6] the principal exponent of this theory.

    Lapse of time does not necessarily mean depreciation.

    Issue between the two schools is question of value.

    Some commissioners, court have taken as test of depreciation that of accountants regardless of whether it is in accord with theory of value. Accountants say depreciation is decline in value, and in their procedure lay down rule for determining annual rate of depreciation, and applying this get present value.

    Economists appeal to market value – market value can't be appealed to in public utilities.

    Straight-line method of depreciation – Accountant took original value, forecast the scrap market value, and divide difference in accounting periods to get depreciation per period. Can this be constant or should the depreciation rate be progressive?

    Cost of production determines value only when there is continuous demand for the good.

    Friday says often necessary to estimate value of public utility not on market value but fitness to render service for which intended.

    Acct. considers cost of new machine scrap value of old, no. of accounting periods. In abandonment of old machine, manager must compare relative economic desirability of old and new machine; this difference gives relative value; then gets two market values of new machine and old as scrap. Value of old plant does not depend on earnings. Valuation of plants for public by commission is more from point of view of manager than from market value. Compare old plant with new.

Conclusion.

Three phases/ideas of depreciation confused:

1. Problem of depreciation as acct. problem
2. Problem of depreciation as economic value
3. Problem of depreciation as public utility policy problem

Dec. 6

Assignment

Marshall – Bk. V, Ch. I, II.
Mill – Bk. III, Ch. II, P. 2, 3, 4, 5.

Consumer's Surplus.

Definition.

Excess of price of that which man would pay over that which he has to pay constitutes consumer's surplus.

> When one conceives of income as gratifications, satisfactions, then Mill's differentiation between productive and unproductive labor will not hold.

> Three ways of measuring income of community.

1. In terms of real commodities
2. In terms of money
   Bowley's accurate per capita estimate
3. In terms of series of gratifications, satisfactions, desirabilities

Consumer's surplus is an endeavor to measure income in terms of utilities, gratifications. Money no approach to measure in terms of satisfactions. Consumer's surplus measures psychic income.

Economist wants to measure in terms of market consumer's satisfaction.

Value in use may be greater than value in exchange. Depuis (?) [probably means Jules Dupuit] began to measure satisfactions in consumer's surplus, and Marshall developed it.

Qualifications of theory.

1. Differences between rich and poor man's income.

>In highly stratified society, money measure of consumer's surplus is a doubtful standard. Because rich man is willing to pay more may simply be because he has more money. More steeply inclined demand curve in highly stratified society.

>Marshall supposes two societies alike as to distribution – people with more steeply inclined demand curve are getting larger total utility and consumer's surplus.

2. Necessaries of Life.

>Consumer's surplus hypothetically infinite. Bernoulli suggests that we shouldn't attempt to measure happiness until we eliminate necessaries. Consumer's surplus begins only when necessaries are satisfied.

Patton's[7] distinction between pleasure and pain economy.

Pleasure economy begins only after pain economy is satisfied.
   Consumer's surplus begins when pleasure economy begins – this is another statement of Bernoulli Theory.

3. Impossibility of measuring consumer's surplus on public goods.

>Can't tell consumer's surplus on park.

>Summary: These three qualification tend to warp demand schedule.

4. More a person spends on anything, the less purchasing power he has for other things (i.e., every fresh expenditure increases marginal value of money to him).

5. Qualification based on articles for ostentation.

Conclusions.

1. Difficulty of getting precise measurement of consumer's surplus.

2. We have some idea of demand schedule within the limits of the variation of supply which have actually occurred.

>High value of diamonds indicate differences in income. Diamonds in inelastic demand. Suppose sudden increase in number of diamonds – consumer's surplus would vanish.

In considering things in middle of scale – the solid comforts of life – wholesome varied food; simplicities of household furniture, houseroom – in considering these solid comforts, there is a real, persistent, consumer's surplus.

Dec. 8

Consumer's Surplus: Its Relation to Diminishing Utility.

Corollaries to principle of diminishing utility similar to consumer's surplus.

1. At either end of scale – i.e., necessities on one hand, and luxurious ostentation on other – consumer's surplus a dubious matter. But in middle of range – solid comforts – there is a real, persistent consumer's surplus.

    Ex. City water supply.

2. Gambling and betting always means loss. One who loses, loses more than the gamer wins, under law of diminishing utility.

3. Prima facie, equality of income brings maximum "human happiness"– same idea as in gambling in (2).

    Here "human happiness" from economic point of view.

    Consumer's surplus – an effort to measure psychic income, human happiness, and therefore, Marshall's analysis of utility. Consumer's surplus, demand curves, etc. and elementary.

Law of Demand and Supply.

Mill's Interpretation.

Equation of supply and demand is equation between quantity wanted and quantity offered at given time.

Law of supply and demands – some one price at which demand and supply are in equilibrium.

Marshall's Interpretation.

Like Mill, in comparison of quantity offered and quantity taken out (apples and apples, corn and corn).

In Mill, articles limited in supply axe those subject to law of supply and demand and no other. Ex. Rare paintings.

Therefore, in Mill, quantity demanded is supposed to vary with price, and quantity offered – supply – fixed.

But Marshall supposes a varying supply as well as demand. Increase of supply on market as price goes up, and supply is decreased as price drops.

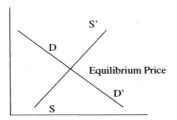

Marshall

Difference between Marshall and Mill lies in fact that supply is fixed – the price at which whole amount will go off. Marshall, on contrary, has flexible supply varying with price.

Which is nearer to facts?

Mill's explanation more in accord with facts and better.

Marshall's way not in accord with facts of market.

Cotton crop, oranges go off at season price.

Price of eggs going down – therefore farmers hurrying eggs to market.

Dec. 10

Treatment of Demand and Supply.

Mill said supply = quantity at a given time.

Marshall said supply variable as well as demand – supply schedule as well as demand schedule. Equilibrium of supply and demand when quantity wanted at Price = quantity carried off at that price <u>at that time</u>.

Bears sell for a fall – want to start others selling to buy again at a lower price. There is a range within which increasing sales will encourage sales, but there is a limit where buying will begin.

<u>Market</u> = region in which uniform price prevails. Ideal market is stock market, cotton or grain market.

Mill considers total supply – for a season for instance

Marshall considers supply at a given time.

Marshall considers flow by which a thing comes to market.

Taussig says Marshall's way of going <u>at it is not</u> in accordance with the facts of the market.

Problem of Market Value – Summary.

Marshallian theory of temporary supply curve positively inclined is not in accord with facts.

Difficult of estimating crops in advance – may be more or less.

<u>Doctrine of Penumbra.</u>

There is penumbra of uncertainty as to

1. Actual supply
2. Demand

At present even more uncertainty than usual.

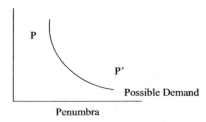

Penumbra

We have an idea of seasonal price at which supply is to go off – within that penumbra the day-to-day fluctuations are <u>not</u> in accordance with Marshallian analysis. Within the limits neither demand nor supply schedule is determinate. (There may be manipulation too.) Therefore, market price within penumbra is indeterminate.

<u>Mill</u> had in mind a <u>seasonal</u> price.

This theory applied to operations of dealers and middlemen – among consumers; there is close accord to regular theory that demand schedule is always negatively inclined.

Present situation affects purchases of consumer's very much as middleman's purchases always are affected – waiting for prices to drop further.

<u>Conclusion.</u>

Mill's statement, properly qualified or stated, answers the theory of demand and supply and market value – fixed seasonal supply – better than Marshallian varying supply.

Assignment

Marshall – Bk. V, Ch. 3.

1. Bk. V, Ch. XIII, Sec. 1, 2 (=Ch. XII, Sec. 1, 2, 3 in 4th ed.).
2. Bk. V, Ch. IV, Sec. 5, 6 (=Sec. 4 in 4th ed.).
3. Bk. V, Ch. V.

Dec. 13

Penumbra Theory.

Region of approximation to seasonal price within which there are conformation to market price. Prices may be in either side of penumbra.
    Significance – Cases where diminishing utility not strictly applicable.
    [In margin, "Application in period of depressions."]
    Economist reasons that in depression lower prices will bring increase demand. Economists err in transferring to immediate conditions theory which are sound in applicability in the long run.
    During depression, wholesalers and retailers buy measly and things move slowly. The larger the depression, the better the accommodation of amount manufactured to consumer's response. The converse happens in period of activity – with rising prices manufacturers, wholesalers, retailers, stock up – then when the things aren't sold as quickly as they anticipate, they slow up.

2. Explains to each for out-of-the-way markets.

Middlemen and manufacturers seek new means of disposing of product without spoiling market and getting people excited. A form of temporary disposing perhaps with concealed price.

3. Reasoning applies more to producers' than to consumers' goods.

Iron, raw wool have desired utility – a longer play of utility – greater scope for penumbra, variability and fluctuations in price.

4. Securities.

Here, diminishing utility theory not strictly applicable. Increase in supply doesn't necessarily mean decline of price – penumbra pretty wide – wider than in iron and steel – here wider than in case of sugar – and sugar penumbra wider than in case of milk.

5. Is demand curve always negatively inclined? Case of Articles of Prestige Value.

Demands and articles of prestige value – increased supply may not bring increased demand. "Advantitous value" [sic] for articles which bring distinction. Some articles sell better if advertised on basis of quality, not price – question involves psychology of consumer.

This a partial explanation in price maintenance business.

Two kinds of Supply Price:

1. Doctrine of penumbra regulates rates at which article comes on market.
2. Other theories affect the increments to stock already in the market.

Law of Substitution (Marshall)

An invention of Marshall's phraseology which has not been accepted. Taussig thinks Marshall never made much of this law of substitution.

Two aspects of laws:

1. Under influence, of law, the cheaper way of production tends to supplant the dearer.
2. Under law, when there are two ways of doing thing, a differential return arises from the more effective, better method.

    Both true – but idea and law have not been a "go."

Cost of Production.

Cost of production = labor, sacrifice, abstinence necessary to bring stock on market.

Supply price = expenses of production = payments necessary to bring stock on market. [in pencil: "minus wages?"]

Yet Marshall goes on to use cost in the Malthusian sense rather than the Ricardian – i.e., in sense of supply price, monetary cost (not sacrifice).

Walker meant monetary cost at hands of no-profits man when he talked of expenses of production.

Marshall meant expenses of production at hands of representative firm – a settled, established firm – much better off than Walker's no-profits man.

Normal Price.

Price brought about by equilibrium of supply price and demand price.

Cairnes' normal price more like Ricardo's natural price. Mill used permanent price.

Cairnes meant about same as Mill and Ricardo – different terminology. Therefore, Cairnes' normal price = Ricardo's natural price = Mill's permanent price.

Marshall says normal price is a relative term dependent on length of period under consideration.

Dec. 17

Normal Price.

Normal price is price which any given set of conditions tends to set up.
    There may be normal price for a day, a season, or secular trend.
    In all there is an equilibrium of supply and demand.
    Persistent price = price which if departed from tends to be returned. There may be aberrations from persistent price at any time, but even so the price will tend to return so long as original conditions of demand and supply remain practically the same.
    Normal price = persistent price which any given set of conditions tend to set up.

Prime and Supplementary Cost.

Prime cost consists of raw materials and labor involved in bringing out the amount of product concerned, i.e., costs which vary directly with quantity produced, within limits.
    Supplementary cost includes appliances, equipment, lay-time salaries, etc., i.e., does not vary directly with quantity produced.

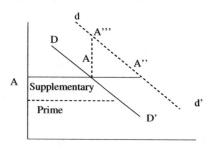

[In margin: "Mill assumes constant cost for intervening period."]

1. Mill would say that temporarily with increase demand high profits to A‴, or ultimately equilibrium at A″ – same price as before.

2. Marshall would agree that A''' short-period normal price. Theory is that prime costs per unit increase; supplementary costs he neglects; but in any case in the intervening period labor inefficient, probably; less careful use of materials etc. – and therefore <u>mounting</u> or increasing supply price, which ultimately goes back to original constant cost as appliances, labor price, etc. are adapted to advanced demand.

In intervening period a succession of equilibria with successive changes in demand. (Like oscillations in market price.)

Marshall's analysis new and attempts to give more realistic interpretation of actual conditions of demand and supply.

Can it be fairly said that there is equilibria of demand and supply in these successive intersections of demand and supply.

Dec. 20

<u>Assignment</u>

Bk. V., Ch. VI.
Bk. IV, Ch. IX, Sec. 7 }
Bk. V, Ch. XII.   } Jan.

<u>Conditions of Constant Cost with Decreased Demand</u>.

Constant cost = Cost irrespective of quantity produced, partly prime, partly supplementary.

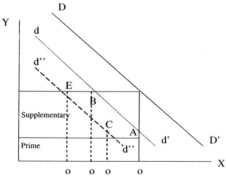

Increase of decrease in demand to d"d"

1. According to Mill, price would drop at once to OA, gradually working up to OE.

2. According to Marshall, drop probably to cir. OB, including same supplementary costs – probably wouldn't get as low as OC for fear of spoiling market.

A succession of points of equilibrium, at any state, there is a point at which price tends to return as long as given conditions last.

Marshall says there is no plain and simple doctrine of theory of value – must be stated with qualifications, explanations, etc.

Three Simple Cases.

1. Constant cost – only inference is to increase quantity produced. Cost of production determines price.

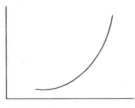

1). Constant

2. Increasing cost.

2. Increasing

3. Decreasing cost.

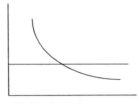

3. Decreasing

Marshall's presentation.

Difficulty in understanding, Marshall – clue lies in his treatment of supply and demand in market day. Marshall concerned in giving doctrine of equilibrium of supply and demand. Preferred this presentation to Mill's simple, bare, and primitive presentation.

Taussig believes it is better to give plain and simple doctrine, and then introduce complications and qualifications.

Marshall's concept of stationary state.

Same as Clark's and Carver's Static State.

Ricardo and Mill meant state to which society was always tending. Society only prevented by improvements in production.

Static State = that in which progress has ceased. Not a hopeless state, as was Mill's and Ricardo's. In latter, returns to laboring class were at barest minimum which would enduce them to go on.

Difference between consumers' and dealers' demand.

Consumers' demand always negatively inclined

Doctrine of penumbra applicable in demand between dealers.

Dec. 22

What Happens to Firm Going at Normal Rate When There Comes Increase in Demand?

1. For a short period, supply curve may not be positively inclined – may even be negatively inclined – perhaps due to slack product, no increase in fixed charges and no great increase in prime cost. Therefore have a kind of equilibrium more like Mill's – market price fixed by equation of supply and demand.

Marshall says equilibrium where supply price = demand price.

Raises question what is normal supplementary price and normal capacity of plant.

U.S. Price Fixing Commission on Iron and Steel fixed price to keep poorest firms going; England met same situation by giving bounty to poorest firms.

Normal capacity.

100% capacity impossible.

90% capacity = maximum and that is abnormal.
80–85% capacity = maximum normal capacity.

Over any period of time. Allow for breakage, etc. Reckon overhead on 80–85% capacity.
Therefore, if demand increased, can increase output without increasing supplementary costs and total cost will decline for time being.

Marshall works out formulae of equilibrium of demand and supply for market price, short- and lay-time normal cost secular cost, etc. And after all this elaboration he gets down to simple doctrine of demand and supply. This treatment due to scientific mind.

Joint and Composite Demand and Supply.

A. Definitions

  1. Derived/demand = demand for commodity used in production of commodity which itself has direct demand.
  2. Composite demand is demand for a substitute – i.e., demand for tea and coffee is a composite demand.
  3. Joint demand is demand for each of several articles jointly demanded for production of commodity which is in direct demand. Demand for house is joint demand for bricklayers, plasterers.

     Joint demand, involves idea of common destination.

  4. Joint supply where production of one inevitably involves production of the other. Coal and gas, cotton and cotton seed. Implies common origin.

     Only one of these phrases which has really established itself is joint supply, which is same as Mill's joint cost.

B. Law of Derived Demand.

  Excess of total demand price over sum of supply prices of other articles. Find derived demand price for window frames by getting demand price minus sum of supply prices for separate commodities involved.

  Packers to get cost of by-products take price they pay for steer, deduct the sum of the demand prices of beef and hides, and difference is cost of by-products.

  Almost no example of joint cost in which there is no separable cost. Only example is cotton seed and cotton lint (?)

Jan. 3, 1921

Assignment

Marshall – Bk. IV, Ch. II, III.

Derived Demand and Supply Prices.

  1. Derived demand price.

> Comes with phenomenon of joint demand. Marshall says subtract from total demand price the supply prices of other constituents. Therefore diff. = derived demand price of constituent in question.

Program.

> Marshall on Equilibrium of Demand & Supply
> "   " Value under Increasing Returns.
> "   " Value under Decreasing Returns.

Value Under Increasing Returns.

  1. External and Internal Economics.

External are those dependent on general improvement of the industry.
  Internal on the organization and efficient management of individual firm.

> Story of wind barometers – Suppose sudden increase in demand which leads to increase in integration of industry, development of ancillary industries, etc.
>
> If through that mere increase in output, *ipso facto*, brings decline in cost, i.e., increasing returns, due to external economics.

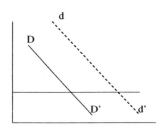

[To right of graph: "Increase of firms and output and development of ancillary industries."]

Query: Is Canada right in claiming she must protect her industries because of greater size of industries of U.S.?

Jan. 8

External and Internal Economies.

Integration of industry is according to Marshall an internal economy.

Meaning of Marshall clearer if he said some improvements resulting in larger output, same in larger scale of production. Former means shifting of demand to right, cause of lower cost.

Improvements which <u>cause</u> increase in output <u>internal</u>

Improvements which <u>result</u> from increase in output <u>external</u>

Ex. Development of ancillary industries, due to slow movement.

Will increase in demand cause internal economies?

It does cause external economies.

If a great many separate establishments recruited to supply output; and there is increase in demand, there will be internal as well as external economics. But where shall number of competing establishments, there is limitation to internal economies (meaning integration chiefly).

<u>Internal economy (integration) leads eventually to monopoly.</u>

Instead of absolute monopoly, large trust may allow a few small concerns to live and sell output at price enabling them to live – but warning vs. increase in number of these small firms.

[Three graphs in the margin]

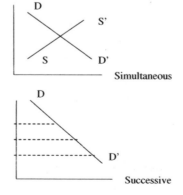

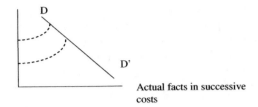

Actual facts in successive
costs

In increasing cost, have simultaneously different costs; in decreasing cost, successively different costs – at given time, firms produce at same cost; with qualifications that improvements are not simultaneously introduced.

Must also qualify simultaneously different costs by saying that this may also hold at <u>successive times</u>.

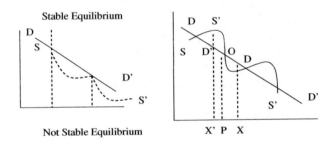

Better draining
OP = stable equilibrium

Long-Period Supply Curves.
   Mill would say that price would be XD and X'D′ at points of unstable equilibrium.

Jan. 10

<u>Assignment</u>

Bk. V, Ch. X, Xi, IX.

<u>Ricardo on Rent.</u>

When he said "Rent is return for original and indestructible powers of soil", he meant to differentiate land from mines which are like reservoie [sic].

Ricardo wrote before the time of Liebig, the protagonist of scientific agriculture. Liebig taught importance of chemical elements of number nitrogen, phosphorus, potash. Manure serves to restore soil. Rotation of crops recent. Restoration of nitrates to soil to put it back to original state.

If constant denudation of soil, it tends to put soil on basis with mines.

Extensive agriculture on the [blank in original] inevitably replaced in time by intensive cultivation.

Liebig's[8] Theory of Niggardly Agriculture.

Used as explanation of the ruined cities of Sicily, Magna Graecia, and countries east of Mediterranean. Robbing soil of productive elements without restoration and predatory cultivation.

Climatologists and meteorologists, etc. question this.

[In margin: Huntington pulse of Asia.]

Changes in industrial centers, ruins of population centers may be due to climatic changes, different precipitation, etc. Therefore Liebig and Agricultural chemists claim there are no original powers of the soil.

Conclusion that inherent qualities of soil are temporary. Is this true?

Marshall on Existence of Indestructible Soils.

Marshall grants that there are indestructible powers of soil – but refers to annuity of air, moisture, sunshine.

Are there permanent differences in the soils?

Marshall would say "dry" faming on the border of 20% precipitation in the west where soil is made to yield more than its apparent potentialities, and this is example of permanent and ineradicable difference in soils – compare Iowa and arid west.

Therefore Marshall would say that this qualification marked original and indestructible powers of soil a little.

Does Marshall say there are often indestructible differences?

Jan. 12

Indestructible Differences in Soils.

1. Annuity of light, air, sunshine, rainfall.
2. Permanent physical differences in soil.

   Dept. of Agriculture makes exhaustive studies of soil to determine deficiencies and virtues in different small sections.

Never make New England hillsides equal to flat, rich soil of Ohio.

Marshall really males too much concession. Doesn't make enough of differences in soils.

Intensive Cultivation on $\left\{\begin{array}{l}\text{Good}\\ \text{\underline{Lands}}\\ \text{Bad}\end{array}\right.$

Most writers claim better returns form intensive cultivation on good lands – can be carried further. This theory, works contra that intensive cultivation tends to wipe out differences in soil.

Therefore, although tendency to wipe out differences is offset by better returns from intensive cultivation on good soils.

Drainage.

Some soils more benefited by removal of superfluous moisture by drainage than others.

Kropotkin's[9] View of Diminishing Returns. $\left\{\begin{array}{l}\text{Value ?}\\ \text{[Blank in original] ?}\end{array}\right.$

[In margin: "Kropotkin: Fields, work-shops, factories."]

Claims possibilities of returns from individual plots hasn't begun to be approached. Optimistic view of philosophical anarchist.

Marshall says Ricardo too nasty in application of diminishing returns – says they didn't make enough allowance for organization.

[In margin: "Value, Physical Quantity"]

Kropotkin views diminishing returns from point of view of value.

Marshall views diminishing returns from point of view of amount

Ricardo views diminishing returns from point of view of amount

Law of diminishing returns as understood by older economists referred only to physical quantity.

If there were no fact of diminishing returns, would there be rent?

Two ways of proving law of diminishing returns.

1. Inductive – laboratory method.

    a. Esslen: Gesietz des abnehmenden Boden vertrages.

       He summarizes accounts of experiments of German agri. status about effect of richly scientific. Chemical agri. Form of tendency of incr. returns to point of maximum returns (optimism) thence diminishing returns – from – point where double dose didn't double product to point where it did nothing.
       Statistical data interesting but not conclusive.
       Tried to prove diminishing returns by direct experiment.

    b. Aroostook County worked out inductive observational, experimental conformation of law.

2. Deductive.

Marshall sees proof of law in acts of farmer.

Jan. 14

Assignment

  1. Bk. V. Ch. VIII, Sec. 5, 6.
  2. Bk. V, Ch. IX.
  3. Bk. V, Ch. XI.

Terminology.

  Rent. (Marshall)
       Producer's surplus equals rent
       Surplus produce
    Term never got wide usage. Rent seems to remain in economic literature.

         Consumer's surplus

         Producer's surplus

Inductive Method.

Used by Germans especially. Leaders were:
       Brentano: Free Trade (Munich)

Schmoller: Berlin

Believed that what now happened in economics understood by going over historical facts.

Schmoller's school didn't adequately interpret facts gathered. Partly due to lack of analytic bent.

Deductive Method.

English tradition has persisted. Kept to Ricardian method. Reasoned deductively about rent.

Marshall reasons that he knows facts because if it weren't so things wouldn't be as they are. People wouldn't be using good and bad soil side by side unless there were diminishing returns – otherwise good land would have driven out bad.

Diminishing Returns.

Theory extremely important to German free-traders. Saw danger of protecting agri. – mean more produced in Germany at higher and higher cost which would mean higher and higher rent.

Ballod[10], German, brought theory of [blank in original] like constant cost up to optimism when sudden increase: thus:

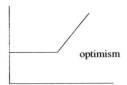

Germans ignorant of Marshallian reasoning and constant cost.

There is indication in this theory ground for statistical study. Perhaps not as sharp as Ballod makes it, – but before sharply diminishing returns there was period of pretty nearly constant return.

[In margin: "Ricardo p. 165"]

Ricardo Underestimates Power, Organization etc.

Marshall forgets theory refers to physical quantity not value of product.

External economics (ies) do work [blank in original] diminishing returns – education, improvements, etc. But circumstance of better market means selling dearer – really here a proof of diminishing returns in terms of quantity.

Distinction between Mines and Agriculture: Indestructible Powers of Soil.

Mines have fixed stores.

Is there law of diminishing returns in both cases?

One is tempted to say _– yes. Same mines richer and yield differential return over poorer.

But in reality law doesn't hold for mines. Law in case of land holds true with each individual plot of land – and holds true of land in general as corollary, or general deduction from law, with regard to each plot.

Of course in mines more trouble as you get deeper – moisture cost higher, water pumping necessary; but also possible that seams get richer and thicker to offset cost. No telling.

[In margin: "Mark Twain Roughing It"]

This is what Ricardo meant in differentiating between rent of mines and rent of agri. soil.

What applies to each plot of land doesn't, apply to each mine. Mines lack sustained phenomenon of increasing pressure as on each plot of land.

Jan. 19

Assignment

[Frank A] Fetter: Passing of the Old Rent Concept. *Q.J.E.*, Vol. 15 (Esp. pp. 445–452, Sec. 5, 6).

Fetter says that by admitting quasi-rents and [end of line here in original]

Jan. 21

Validity of Distinction Between Interest and Rent.

Ricardo said rent didn't enter into cost of production. George always claimed rent, i.e., unearned increment – was at base of social evils.

Marshall begins question of this distinction and its validity.

1. Marshall claims land is fixed, and capital flexible.

   Objection is that land is not at all a fixed quantity to economist, who though admitting area of earth is fixed, says the land available for economic purposes is not a fixed quantity. Add to land surface by improvements of transportation (ex. [blank in original] non-existent economically 50 years ago) by process of change (especially in cases of urban sites). In mineral resources where great possibilities of extensibility (Day's paper shows Index of Physical Product from Mines).[11]

Fetter claims available supply of land can be diminished by man's action. Therefore Taussig questions if Marshall's position on this point is not open to attack.

Peculiarities of Marshallian Analysis.

1. Supposition of War in England.

   Will make applications to secure improvements – intensive cultivation to secure maximum return over period of war. Return from short-period improvements = ? Interest Return from long-period improvements = ? Quasi-rent.

2. Suppositions of meteoric stones.
   a. Stones all fallen and all found therefore fixed supply.
   b. Stones all fallen but not all found therefore irregular supply with slow increase.
   c. Stones easily and quickly found and reproduced at constant cost. Regular, calculable, short-period constant cost.

   Marshall says these examples of true rent, quasi-rent, interest.

Sub-soil drainage.

Man who at beginning of war had drainage system which increased his production would get quasi-rent, whereas man whose drainage system was permanently more effective would get true rent.

   Bk. VI. Ch. IX. Essential Difference Between Rent – Quasi-rent – Interest, Sec.5 (p. 635).

      ? Replacibility [sic]

      ? Does landlord get rent and quasi-rent and undertaker interest?

Jan. 24

Phraseology of Marshall.

> Quasi-rent has been pretty generally accepted (external and internal eco-
> nomics less so: substitution not at all)
>
> Relation to prime cost, supplementary cost, total cost.
>
> Prime cost enters into short-time price, supplementary doesn't.
>
> What you receive in excess of prime cost.
>
> [Undecipherable graph here]
>
> Quasi-rent is result of price for short period.
>
> Quasi-rent is excess over and above what is necessary for time-being to
> keep you going.
>
> Rent is excess over total cost which for long periods you must get to
> keep on.
>
> Therefore Marshall says quasi-rent is excess above prime costs which is
> as necessary to continuance of business as prime costs.
>
> Marshall says that price under these circumstances is determined by
> equilibrium of supply and demand.

N.B. Difference Between Rent, Quasi-Rent, Interest.

Landlord molds long-time improvements. Over long time, there are equalizing
tendencies which prevent returns from improvements becoming over-great or
over-small.

Farmer supplies short-time improvements – manure, etc. therefore he gets
interest. And what he pays to landlord is rent and quasi-rent.

> Rent   Quasi-Rent | Interest

Therefore line of cleavage is between interest and quasi-rent.

(Rent doesn't affect price and for long periods quasi-rent does.)

Mill talked of improvements sunk in soil though he didn't call it quasi-rent.

Mill and George would have put line of cleavage between rent and quasi-rent.

Marginal Costs in Relation to Urban Values.

Marshall sees here a third class. Von Thünen's rent of composite origin – (1)
fertility and (2) location.

Value of rates in N.Y.C. due largely to custom – Wall Street might as well be East or West of Broadway. Docks due to natural reasons, but not Wall St.

Marshall means that causes which affect rent are partly man-made and partly entirely beyond man's control. Ordinarily causes which makes city lands valuable are beyond man's control. Therefore income from urban sites is not fixed by causes which can be analyzed as natural or physical.

Even with railways, proximity to railroad is physical cause. And there are physical causes for value of sites in N.Y.C. But these physical causes are minor as of. The human element. In case of agri. land, investment by owner and intention of grower important; but not so much on urban land.

Jan. 26

Marshall on Pioneers.

Settler in new country takes risk and hardships with expectation of use of value of land. Discussion active in eighties and nineties in England. Agri. prices fell and it was ascribed to overseas interest – over foreign competition. Tariff of 1892 in response to this overseas competition and fall in agri. prices. Free-trader says O.K. or "it isn't so bad, it won't last."

This Marshall's attitude – says pioneer stage is temporary and peculiarly acute, because in pioneer state crop is in nature of a by-product. For what owner wants is he is looking for future development. Therefore Marshall says inundation of products from pioneer country is temporary. Ultimately pioneer will be subject to ordinary conditions.

Something to it – Marshall overstates case.

Is this return rent or quasi-rent?

Marshall says accretion value is in sense return for risk and not to be viewed as unearned increment. When land is settled, then return will be rent – i.e. result, not cause of price.

Marshallian Terms.

Composite Rent.
    May be based on sense of

1. Rent of parcel real estate (land and building together)
2. In case of combination of factions which together bring true rent – (ex. Dock site plus influx of trade to that general location)
3. Used in sense of composite rent of business ability and business site – particularly observable in retail trade. Man builds up business on ability and site. Ex. Shuman's Corner on Washington and Summer Streets.

In general, term hasn't been a "go"

Pullman and Saltaire[12]

Due to undertaker's ability and energy.

> {Urban land = men-made causes.
>
> {Agri. land = not man-made causes.
>
> Interest equals return from man-made causes.
>
> Element of risk important in establishing a city as seen in Depew, N.Y.

Establishment of railroads involved land speculation.

This process of directly, deliberately trying to direct process of urban growth is extremely risky. If less risky it would be more common. Some succeeded; Depew failed.

Marshall would call it quasi-rent.

Not certain of definite connection of returns to expenditure.

Urban Site Rent.

> How divide between rent and quasi-rent.
> 1. Gold Coast at Harvard – lost prestige with upper classmen and also with building of freshman dormitory.
> 2. Richardsonian Architecture and its Emphasis on Romanesque – now supplanted by modern steel buildings with little wall and much light.

(Note: Rent included urban as well as agricultural rent.)

> Differential value on site determined by higgling of market. Suppose site worth $100,000 because man knows how to use the site for appropriate building. If man builds Richardsonian building = $100,000.
>
> Minimum which will be accepted before he gives it up is yield on value of site with nothing on it.
>
> Marshall would say that excess over what site would yield bare is quasi-rent.
>
> Site rent is comparable to prime cost, and anything above necessary part of supplementary cost is quasi-rent.
>
> Ex. Houses on Mass. Ave. where yield greater than return on site alone.

<u>Second Semester</u>

Feb. 14

<u>Assignment</u>

<u>Marshall</u> – Ch. 13 – Theory of Changes of Supply and Demand with references to doctrine of maximum satisfaction.

<u>Quasi-Rent in Application to Urban Sites.</u>

Quasi-rent works both ways – in bad and good luck. May come from cessation of demand as well as increased demand.

   Structures are put on urban site which will yield greatest differential gains – rain represents special gain. Older economist saw only working out of supply to meet demand – fail to consider failures in return from poor investment. Marshall says quasi-rent can be reckoned in excess of what he would get at minimum.

I.

Building cost	$100,000
Land $3000 @ 6%	50,000
"Normal value"	150,000
Normal rental	9,000
Actual rental	4,500
Actual value	75,000

II.

New Building	$100,000)	$6000)	
Lose on old			) – $10,500
bldg.	75,000)	4500)	
Total outlay	175,000 -------		rental $9,000

III.

Rise in rent	)
Rise in land value	) To total rental = $12,000.

Until conditions under III will come only with urban development and not until then will old building be torn down.

These conditions common in urban development – so much as one would expect aleatory element to be allowed for. Only really shrewd men make money out of real estate.

George's reasoning assumes sharply defined accruing unearned increment. Quasi-rent theory doesn't allow this sharp demarcation.

Aleatory element very important – buildings decrease in value, become obsolete. Tenants not charged for obsolescence and depreciation.

Experiments in Increment Taxes.

1. German increment taxes
2. Adams experiment in 1909

Very uncertain measures both in practice and effect. This links up directly with quasi-rent theory.

Feb. 16

Assignment

Marshall – Bk. VI, Ch. 4, 5.

> Book IX deals with Supply, Book V, with Demand, and Book VI their application to distribution.

Theory of Changes of Supply and Demand with Reference to Doctrine of Maximum Satisfaction.

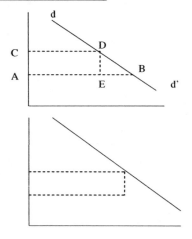

I. Tax

CDEA = amount of tax
CDBA = amount of decrease in consumer's supply

DEB = excess of decrease in c.s. our tax

Conclusions: In either case you lose more in consumer's surplus than the amount of tax or bounty.

B. <u>Increasing Cost</u>.

[Indecipherable graph in original text]

   EDAC = decrease in consumer's surplus therefore whether tax exceeds decrease in c.s. depends on relation between ΔDBC (#1) and ABFG (#2). This relation depends on inclination of supply curve.

   There will be recession of m. of cultivation.

   Amount of tax may exceed loss in c. surplus.

Qualifications of consumers' surplus.

1. Differences in wealth
2. Prestige value
3. Necessities = infinite c.s. [consumer surplus]
4. Conventional necessities.

C. <u>Decreasing Cost Case.</u>

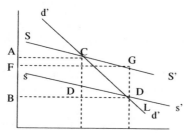

ACEB = incr. in cons. surplus
FGEB = amount of bounty which in the case is less than increase in consumer's surplus

I. Bounty

   Amount of increase in c.s. > bounty

<u>Conclusions</u>.

If community taxes commodity produced under diminishing returns and a bounty on commodity produced under increasing returns, there is always net gain.

<u>Applicability of Theory of Consumer's Surplus</u>.

One of most devious qualifications to theory is the differences in wealth, which changes m[arginal] utility of money to rich and poor.

Same qualification holds in theory of applicability of taxes and bounties in increasing and decreasing cost.

It is a "final analysis" as Marshall calls it – it is not elementary. Is it <u>practical</u>? Or is it an intellectual plaything?

Feb.18

<u>Assignment</u>

<u>Marshall</u> – Bk. VI, Sec. 3, 4, 5.

Does Marshall think there are non-competing group?

<u>Doctrine of maximum Satisfaction</u>.

Pt. of maximum satisfaction from accruing dividend – i.e., <u>consumer's doctrine</u>.

Hedonistic view looks on mechanical satisfaction. Therefore this doctrine is a consumer's doctrine.

Marshall's theory of maximum satisfaction is that if you let people alone – laissez-faire – they will get maximum satisfaction. Therefore this is justification of system of freedom in enterprise.

> This idea underlies Webb's idea of Fabian Utopia sketched in his new book.

> This doctrine not doctrine of political or governmental laissez-faire – idea simply that freedom of choices further limits – narcotics, liquor, opium, tends to bring maximum satisfaction.

Marshall goes on to say that inequality of income modifies idea of maximum satisfaction. This is not real qualification of theory. But given inequality of income, way to get maximum satisfaction is still to let people spend money as they please.

But the qualification which Marshall does introduce is that you may increase maximum satisfaction by interference in such a way as to tax articles produced under diminishing returns and give bounty on things produced under increasing returns – thus decreasing production of former and increasing production of latter.

> If you follow this rule with [blank] choice of commodities on which you place and those on which you give bounty. Only successful if it brings increased returns through external economics: then slowly, with iron-bound consistency, carry out program, perhaps increase satisfaction.

But as political program it would probably never work out. Really theory is little more than an intellectual plaything. Objections from administrative point of view are insuperable, much greater than theoretical objections.

>There are other ways of increasing consumer's satisfaction, i.e. by education (ex. increase satisfaction from good music constantly heard).

Consumer's surplus doesn't rest on idea of equality of income; but   inequality of income does introduce a qualification in measuring consumer's surplus – i.e., converting money c.s. into consumer's satisfaction. For instance, if incomes were equal, what people would pay for price of ticket to Kreizler concert gives accurate measure of c.s.

Out on Feb. 21

Difference in Wages.

Feb. 23

Peculiarities of Labor.

Cumulative character of some – more cumulative character of others.

Analogy: 1. With caste system in India, the longer it lasts, the less arbitrarily drawn.
        2. Tare system in which tenant shares proceeds. Tenant receives advances from landlord which are charged to him at harvest and deduction made. This, like caste system, is non-cumulative. It tends to break down.

Peculiarities.

I. Those who train laborer do not receive reward. Therefore things which would naturally be done are not because someone else gets reward.

>Ex. Domestic servants. Apprentice schools. This peculiarity far-reaching in its effects. Introduces a peculiarity in progress of mankind in matter of investment in "immaterial capital" of community. This peculiarity is cumulative in its effects.

>This involves problem of wages for [blank] stratum in society – requires long effort to bring the "submerged tenth" up to point of being valuable members of society. But this will never be done on commercial

principles – necessitates altruism. But up to now it hasn't paid and therefore it hasn't been done.

II. Immobility, perishable character of labor: Lack of Resev.

Led Marshall to application of quasi-rent theory to labor.

See apostolic succession in diff. in wages through South, Ricardo, Mill,
Cairnes to Marshall.

Can imagine system of equalizing differences in wages, difference
between hard handed and soft handed jobs.

III. Long training necessary: Hard to predict demand.

Marshall's position on difference in wages.

Bk. VI, Ch. 5, Sec. 6 – see pp. 576–577
Cf. p. 514 – Bk. XI, Ch. 1, Sec. 6.

(p. 576 – Doctrine of cost of production determining learning and training in long
run wages. P. 514 – Refers to non-competing groups.)
   Reciprocal demand determining wages.
   Cairnes doesn't consider differences in standard of living in different groups.
[Blank] merely on reciprocal demand.
   Marshall intimates different supply price within group, based on standard of
living.

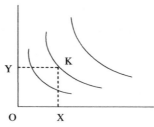

XK equal long-period supply price – price may change with increase and
decrease of demand but essentially comes back to KX as permanent equilibrium,
based on standard of living.
   But Marshall doesn't mean equalization of standard of living between groups –
each group will have its own supply price.

Assignment

Bk. IV, Ch. 12, Supply of Business Mt.

Feb. 25

<u>Differences in Wages</u> (cont)

P. 577. Leaving out human agenda and referring only to machines and material agents, the word "equal" might be substituted for "sufficient"; therefore the word "sufficient" conceals a reservation – implication that rewards are not equal, and that "sufficient" means difference in standard of living, and reward must be sufficient to maintain standard and allow for reproduction. Must you pay different rewards in return for efforts and sacrifices? This the great, crucial question – and Marshall dodges the problem by use of word "sufficient".

Early edition says that what determines remuneration in different groups is <u>not</u> determined by reciprocal demand but by standard of living of different groups – i.e. <u>cost of production of laborers</u>. Demand effective only insofar as that if there were no demand here would be no laborers in that group – or demand determines number of laborers in group.

Three ways of expanding theory –

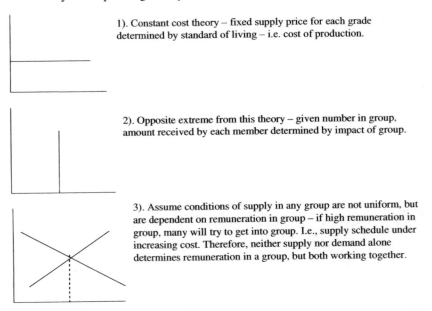

1). Constant cost theory – fixed supply price for each grade determined by standard of living – i.e. cost of production.

2). Opposite extreme from this theory – given number in group, amount received by each member determined by impact of group.

3). Assume conditions of supply in any group are not uniform, but are dependent on remuneration in group – if high remuneration in group, many will try to get into group. I.e., supply schedule under increasing cost. Therefore, neither supply nor demand alone determines remuneration in a group, but both working together.

Marshall intimates in second edition that conditions he has in mind, that he has in mind conditions under #1 – but he [blank] off and qualifies this, as seen in p. 514.

Industrial Organization. Business Management.

Is Marshall's Theory Like Walker's?

Marshall says strong firm doesn't remain in possession of same family. If one inherits father's ability, it will probably remain in family – if not, it won't. No Kidder, no Peabody, in Kidder Peabody.[13] Morgans more like hereditary dynasty. Walker would say it is because son doesn't inherit his father's ability. Marshall admits possibility of continuation of ability but diversion ability into other fields – professions, callings.

Bk. VI, Ch. 7–8
Next week: Clark: Distribution of Wealth.

Mar. 2

How Much is a Man Worth: Reward vs. Services.

By successive steps, – compare firemen in terms of men: division superintendent with firemen, superintendent with division superintendent and finally on up to manager – but it would be impossible to make direct comparison between laborer and manufacturer. This is process of gauging the services via the intermediate steps.

Walker had same idea in his types of businessmen, from no-profits employer to the "midas – undertaker."

Possibility of Failure of Adjustment of Services and Rewards.

Especially in case of pioneers and inventors. Tried to be kept in control of businessmen. Path breakers, ahead of their time, didn't get reward in proportion to services.

Characteristic of Marshall to put qualifications first. Should have put principle first:

1. Remuneration in proportion to sacrifice
2. Remuneration in proportion to efficiency

Marshall says it may at first seem impracticable to set earnings and service against each other in business profits. But by successive comparisons he does it

P. 622: Proportion of Time Earnings of Effort: Larger Part of Profits of Business Man is Quasi-Rent.

Why? (Return later)

P. 313: Business Ability Has Fairly Defined Supply Price.

What kind of supply price?

> I.e., Supply price for any particular grade of ability.
>
> Constant Cost? I.e., Can you get as many as you want at given price?
>
> Increasing Cost? Added supplies at higher cost?

[In margin: "See Bk. VI, Ch. 12, Sec. 11"]

The earnings of exceptional ability are rising, which accentuate relative fall of incomes earned by moderate ability. This is due to two causes:

1. General growth of matter.
2. New facilities for communication by which men can apply constructive or speculative genius.

> #1 acts almost alone in professional incomes, while both act fully with regard to business incomes.

Mar. 4

Quasi-Rent is Larger Part of Profits of Business Man.

To get quasi-rent of urban site – get estimate of site rent, subtract rental, and difference equals quasi-rent. When he goes down to site rent and no more, he'll let building go. If owner of factory gets anything on prime cost, he'll probably stick to it. With small grocer, corner drug store, the aleatory (?) character of business is most striking. The inexorable minimum here is greater part of earning than in case of business man to whom Marshall refers. With him the "inexorable" minimum is small part of total income.

Concept of Composite Quasi-Rent.

Business man has "organization" to which considerations of this sort apply. Good many workers get an excess over what is necessary to keep them there. How share composite quasi-rent in bad times? Probably prefer to accept temporary reduction of wages than quit. Composite quasi-rent equals gain of excesses of different employees over minimum which employees will take rather than quit. Division of [blank] reducing of quasi-rent in bad times occasion for conciliation rather than arbitration.

Here taking about quasi-rent of individual. May get quasi-rent from year to year but may not get any over period of time.

Marshallian theory of business profits is theory of risk not only for individuals but for class. Class takes risks also – never any telling how things will turn out either for individual or class. (Like copper and gold mining). Can't tell at beginning who has the real stuff in him. Therefore business profits are part of what you must pay to get people to enter into project.

So far as individual is concerned, rent theory holds; not for trade as whole, a part of cost. Therefore rent theory not applicable. Exceptional earnings as far as class is concerned is quasi-rent – not time rent (i.e. differential return Whish doesn't enter into supply price).

Successful opera singer's returns analogous – must have good voice which won't go to pieces, dramatic ability, long and arduous training; many try who never succeed. No accident that some are successful – only can't find who has ability without trying.

> Query: What do you think or it
>
> What does logic of thing hinge on?

Mar. 7

Marshall would say that when due allowance is made for successes and failures, there is no surplus which doesn't enter into the supply price, necessary to secure the necessary ability. Therefore profits do enter into cost of production and, contrary to Walker's idea, are not rent when viewed from point of view of whole class or trade.

(Note: This is not risk theory of profits which Hawley enumerates. Says entrepreneur always gets return for risk. Therefore not Marshall's theory of offsetting of successes and failures. Hawley might think everyone could succeed and still hold risk theory.)

Two methods of approach and verification to question:

1. Inductive statistical approach.

   Take 10,000 examples and balance to see proportionate number of successes and failures.

2. Ascertain its accord with familiar facts by observation.

   Deductive method.

Bastiat, great free-trader and defender of rights of private property in France in middle of 19th century. (See "Petition to the Candle-Makers.")

Bastiat denied rent theory. Not in accord with economic harmony. Argued thus: once in a while there seems to be large increment in nature of rent, nevertheless it doesn't generally hold.

Compare copper and coal mining – pretty easy to know somewhere near what you are going to get in coal mining. Element of risk very different here from copper mining.

Element of risk in land vastly less – can pretty well predict quality and potential yield of land – than in case of factory building, choice of site, business prospects, etc. Bastiat wrong in emphasis on element of risk in agricultural land. Chose [blank in original] example in vineyard in which there is risk.

> Two questions:
> 1. Is fatal p.c. as great as Marshall says?
> 2. Does mortality act as deterrent to others?
>   Marshall says 90% in answer to #1.
>   In regard to #2 we are peculiarly in the dark.
>   Admitting great mortality (say 50%, and perhaps greater in business than anywhere else), does it act as deterrent?
>   Usually question of temperament. Taussig says the midases, the exceptionally able, are never deterred by failure of others.
>   Question different from this below – i.e., the solid businessmen – problem more complex.
>   What can be said for them not only as to risk, but whole problem of non-competing groups? Does Marshall's reasoning of supply price concluding allowance for failure apply here?

Mar. 9

Assignment

Clark – Distribution of Wealth, Ch. 7, 8

Biologists – hometrists, Salton and Pearson have called attention to some interesting aspects of question of heredity, i.e.

1. Inter-class differences vs. Infra-class differences.

   Differences between individuals which perpetuate themselves while species remains about same. (Evolutionary changes)

Applicability of theory to Non-Competing Groups.

1. Differences between individuals in any class are unmistakable.
2. Question is: are there ineradicable <u>inter-class</u> differences?

   Involves question – what is basis of social stratification. It is a phenomena which reasserts itself in all stages of or civilization – feudalism, Hindu caste system, Manchu dynasty in China, etc.

Chauncy says N.E. community of 17th century started stratified – not at beginning even a homogeneous group. Rather a cross-section of English society at that time. Yet here at that time not lack of opportunity to rise.

Explanation of social stratification.

1. Are there inter-class differences in endowments.
2. Is it due to artificial obstacles which prevent movement from class to class.

Application to businessmen who occupy place in "upper tier" – well-to-do.

1. Are they persons of superior endowment.
2. Is their advantageous position due to opportune circumstances in command of capital, education, social position?

An unsolved question. Biometric evidence throws light only on infra-class differences, not on inter-class differences. At present state of knowledge, we don't know.

Marshall doesn't face this fundamental question – has it in mind, but doesn't present it fairly or squarely.

Ross' treatment of social stratification from standpoint of manifestations of social stratification; but doesn't face or even point out the main problem.

(Mills saw underlying social question – why was there absence of competition; Cairnes saw mechanism therefore Mill saw more of problem than Cairnes)

In business profits, the factitious, environmental factors count for less in business than in almost any other occupation of well-to-do. Law, medicine, etc. much more influenced by such factors. Therefore, environmental difficulties less important, and inborn abilities count for more. Yet it is true that although leading businessmen are self-made in sense that they start poor, yet they often come from upper middle, better situated class.

In U.S., American farmer offers puzzling phenomenon. Lots of farmers sons climb up. American farmer does manual work, but very spry, ambitious – therefore different from ordinary laboring class.

Another Phase of Question of Social Stratification.

Are there non-competing groups?

<u>Cairnes</u> thought shifting between groups negligible. Not strange to think so in England. Lines between classes drawn very taut. Tending now to disintegrate, but leas so than in U.S. Social classes here disintegrating.

<u>Objections to non-competing groups from two standpoints.</u>

1. Differences within groups are enormous.
2. Groups aren't sharply separated.

But though it is true that it is easy to advance up one or two rungs in ladder, but to say there is free movement From top of bottom of (social) ladder is exaggeration.

   <u>There are differences other then equalizing differences</u>; but whether due to inter-class or infra-class differences we do not know.

Mar. 11

Clark: Distribution of Wealth.

Clark started as clergyman. Smith, Columbia, Carnegie Foundation for Peace. Wrote in two books on Static Economics – intended to write on dynamics but probably will not.

   Also wrote "[Blank] of Economic Theory".

   "Distribution of Wealth" deals with statics of economics. In use of "natural" price, etc. a harking back to older economists. He means, however, by natural laws not what Adam Smith did – i.e., <u>an order</u> of nature, with teleological, perhaps theological implications – Clark means <u>normal</u> state – i.e., place to which things, if departed from, tended to return. Clark speaks of it as no-profits state.

   In no-profits state, rent, interest, wages, but no profits which occur only in dynamic state. Therefore in static state, returns to entrepreneur on wages. In dynamic state with changes, some men get ahead of others and enjoy differential gain. No quasi-rent in static state – and no business profits in Walker's differential sense.

   In static state, not only settled conditions, but it is frictionless state – differences [blank in original]. If one man gets more wages than another, due to permanent causes. A good deal like Ricardo's frictionless state. Advantage of such state's treatment in that it centers attention on fundamental laws.

Theory of Wages.

1. Clark cites Adam Smith's statement that in early society, laborer got whole product of his labor; and by shows impossibility of separating labor from capital in modern industry therefore difficult to distinguish the specific product of labor.

2. George says wages in static state must correspond to returns to worker on free land.

   a Criticizes this by saying condition of free land only a transitional state, not a normal condition therefore puts squatter in strategic position – not enough of him.

   b. Also says large part of homesteader's income is accruing rent from increasing value of land and which was inducement to him to settle.

(Marshall's theory of deferred payments – use in value must be regarded as part of price in order to induce homesteader to take risk of hardship.)

So Clark says homesteader gets composite income in which rent is included therefore even if there enough squatters, wouldn't use his income for getting basis for wages.

Clark says there are marginal regions in which wages are determined. But no-rent land not sufficiently wide bases therefore includes no-rent machines.

<u>Zone of indifference</u> is zone in which it makes no difference to employer whether workers continue or not.

1. <u>Extensive zone of indifference</u> applied to increase of machinery, where there are wages but no interest – capital, but no return to capital. (Extensive margin of cultivation – return all goes to laborer – no return in nature of rent.)

2. <u>Intensive zone of indifference</u> when applied to machinery point where it does not pay entrepreneur to make further application of labor to existing plant therefore no return to capital – labor gets all produced. (So with land – all returns go to labor, and there is no rent.)

Here Clark makes application of intensive and extensive margin of cultivation of land theory to industry.

In this way he gets back to original theme in which he says George was on right track but went at it in wrong way. In George's theory zone of indifference is relatively negligible – as vs. Wide zone by Clark's concept.

Mar. 14

<u>Assignment</u>

Ch. IX (omit 158–139)
Ch. XVIII, pp. 267–275
Ch. XX

Clark's "Zone of Indifference."

Analogous to Walker's no-profits stage, but Walker's stage includes return to capital whereas Clark's zone of indifference does not. Also, former presupposes dynamic state; Clark's reasoning based on static state.

Point at which zone of indifference will settle is determined by relation between supply of capital and supply of laborers.

Firms will differ in policy of using machines – some will keep up machinery to A-1 condition all the time, taking cost of depreciation as it goes along; some will use steadily, not bother much with repair, and discard when it is worn out. Latter polity more common where obsolescence a factor – but obsolescence not important in static state.

Clark ignores differences in wages – ignores non-competing groups, social stratification. Like Ricardo in this.

Clark lumps rent and interest – "property income" as different from "labor income". This concept in speaking of no-rent instrument. (Also no distinction between land and capital.)

Static State

No friction. No dynamic change. Mobility of labor and capital.

Clark's illustrations of outworn capital "unstylish goods" doesn't belong to the static state.

If 105 men can run factory better than 100 men, and if difference of output equals wages of those five men, they are on zone of indifference.

Mar. 16

Zone of Indifference. (cont.)

Extensive zone of indifference doesn't apply to static state. (Pretty good argument vs. existence of extensive zone in static state.)

We presuppose that manager knows what laborers are getting returns equal to the specific product of labor.

Is the one of indifference, –whether a point, a line or a broad zone – ever reached? And if reached, is it a zone (not settled), line, or point? I.e., is there or is there not a zone of indifference?

Capital vs. Capital Goods.

Term "capital goods" has been "a go".

Usefulness of distinction lies in its application.

1. Capital is permanent; capital goods transitory

    As used by Clark, means capital value

    Value of capital may be identical with value of capital goods.

2. Capital is mobile, capital goods aren't.

3. Capital has no definite identity; capital goods have. Forms of crystallized value differ.

4. Capital yields interest; capital goods yield rent.

    Here Clark is asserting that old distinction between rent and interest doesn't hold.

    Land and machines both capital goods.

5. Capital goods reproduce themselves as they go along; capital involves original abstinence, i.e., abstinence originates capital.

    Supposed that competition brings it about that there is even rate of return from instruments of production.

    Is this distinction valid – or is there abstinence to have capital goods reproduced?

    If 100% inheritance tax were imposed would capital be maintained?

6. Capital goods have periods of production; capital doesn't – works incessantly.

Assignment

Clark – Ch. 11, 12, 13, 21

Capital and Capital Goods.

Clark claims that capital involves abstinence – incr. capital only by abstinence?

Question not answered in class.

Relation of Capital to Wages.

Capital a reservois which makes waiting unnecessary therefore it acts as bridge by which it is possible for laborer to be paid out of current labor. Therefore no advances to laborers, and no waiting. Clark assumes stock of capital goods and product at various points (stages) of production:

A	B	—	H
A′	B′	—	H′
A″	B″	—	H″
A‴	B‴	—	H‴

Clark admits abstinence at <u>beginning</u>.

Clark's theory means that capital deserves interest not because it involves abstinence but because it is productive. This therefore hits the established line of theory. This theory that labor is immediately rewarded with no delay, no advances is logically tied up with Clark's theory that there is no abstinence in creation of capital goods, i.e., they reproduce themselves automatically.

Mar. 21

<u>Clark's Theory of Synchronizing of Labor and Capital.</u>

<u>Mill</u> would say that wages are advanced by capitalist to laborer and Clark, p. 805, profits are caused by laborer earning more than is turned over to him (wage-fund doctrine). Therefore Mill would disagree with Clark's idea that it was not a question of relation between capital and labor, but between subgroup of laborers.

<u>Böhm-Bawerk</u> says we use capitalistic in two senses:

1. Capitalistic in sense of inequalities of wealth – capitalists being possessing class.
2. Technical sense – community equipped with elaborate capitalistic outfit. Operations of productions in successive stages.

Older economists meant <u>capitalistic</u> in sense of #1.

In their analysis, capitalists and laborers included in groups, A, A′, A″, A‴; and problem of these subgroups entirely separate. Those in A‴ produce more than they are in need of. Would say interrelations between subgroups very complex. Also they would say that order of production is not

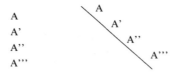

They would say synchronizing of labor add capital is moonshine. Taussig agrees.

Suppose a society socialistically inclined but in technical sense (see preceding page) capitalistic. Would there be advances? If there were, they would be different in character and consequence than under capitalistic system.

If at any moment a cooperative society (community) took account of stock, there would be a supply of finished goods. If by advance you mean process which means continuance of capitalistic system in technical sense, this is entirely different from advance in possessive capitalistic sense.

As to question of advances, older economists were right. Those who have advance to those who have not. Entirely different question from question of justice or injustice of inequalities of   distribution.

The Specific Product of Labor and Capital.

Final Productivity Theory.

The specific product, which is effectively final product – the laborer gets its specific product, the capital gets its specific product.

Distinction between capital and capital Goods

1. Capital is permanent, capital goods not.
2. Capital is permanently embodied in capital goods, capital goods change their form.

According to Clark, if capital is increased, product is increased; wages rise, interest falls.

(See: Carver, Ch. II, pp. 65–76, 216–224)
(Böhm-Bawerk – *Q.J.E.* XII, 247)

Mar. 23

Assignment

Marshall – Bk. VI, Ch. I, Sec. 7, 8, 9.

Suppose Constant Supply of Labor and Addition of Successive Increments of Capital.

First dose brings large returns; second dose adds less than first, and so on. Total product increased with each dose, but at decreasing rate. This is universal law of diminishing returns.

Suppose constant quantity of capital, and increase in supply of laborers. It will be reverse of the same process.

> At margin is there joint product of both labor and capital, one thing specific product of labor, other of capital, or only one, according to which is constant?

> Specific product of capital equals interest.

> Specific product of labor equals wages.

What does Clark mean by margin? Does he get margins of capital and labor by different processes or same?

Difficulty with theory that there is joint product of both labor and capital is to harmonize it with zone of indifference.

Can there be zone of indifference with regard to labor, i.e., point where everything goes to capital, nothing to labor? Labor would die off!

Mar. 25

Marshall's Position in Marginal Productivity. Zone of Indifference, etc.

1. Returns to Labor

   Wages of any group of laborers tend to equal net product of marginal laborer of group. But this isn't, he says, a theory of wages (Does this mean it isn't valid, or that it isn't predictable?)

   > Dynamic condition equals conditions in which there is not only continuing friction and movement, but continual causes of friction. Things move.

   Marshall, like Clark considers quantity of labor and capital etc.

   Marshall assumes normal efficiency [blank in original]. Marshall thinks capital is of labor and waiting. This would upset Clark's theory of abstinence.

2. Zone of indifference

   Marshall says net product of marginal man determines wages of group. Marshall's margin has "family resemblance" to Clark's zone. Marshall's "margin of doubt" less sharply defined than Clark's zone – what man dose, i.e., whether he lives or doesn't live – man on margin of doubt Marshall doesn't say.

   Marshall holds old doctrine that operations of capitalist are resolvable into a succession of advances. (Taussig agrees.)

Marshall says can't call marginal man's net return a theory of wages, because one can't record all other expenses of production. Marshall's idea of marginal man of a grade or class determining wages for class has in mind non-competing groups. This wouldn't involve circular reasoning. But disregarding non-competing groups (which Marshall shoved tendency to throw over) and treating of general wages can't apply productivity theory.

Mar. 26

Application of Principle of Diminishing Returns to Labor and Capital.

Carver's example of added [blank] in factory could indicate law of diminishing returns sharply active.

Clark would say diminishing returns active not as you increase number of instruments but improve quality of instruments – in Ricardian language, as you increase quantity of previously embodied labor.

But (Taussig says) though it looks as it improvements would continue, is it predictable? Is there any law about it? For last 100 years diminishing returns probably not apparent.

By removing dynamic element, and assume increase in capital goods resulting from increased capital, will there or will there not be sharply diminishing returns?

1. Reduced rate of interest will bring in more and more capital goods, many of them familiar, which would add to product at the [blank] less rate. But how do we know this? Prove by the "grand style – deductive reasoning. Method used by Böhm-Bawerk [blank] and explained – says reason that if rate of interest goes down, there are good many worthwhile improvements to make. Two reasons we don't use these old, familiar improvements.

    1. We know new better ways

    2. Rate of interest not low enough to warrant it.

Question: How wide a play for this increase of capital goods?

[In margin: "See Taussig: Principles of Interest"] Surely wider than Carver indicates in discussing mere duplication of existing instruments.

Good deal of uncertainty, Taussig says.

Conclusions.

Fairly apparent tendency to stability, uniformity in rate of interest. Do some utilizations of capital continue to be better than others. In Clark's view are all units of capital equally productive. What happens at margin? (See Ch. 21)

Mar. 20

Assignment

Böhm-Bawerk – *Q.J.E.* XXI, p. 247.

Two Phases of Addition of Increments.

> Labor and Capital.
>
> Is there one margin for labor and one for capital? Are all units of each equally productive?
>
> Clark connects business profits with dynamic conditions.
>
> Is Clark's reasoning about marginal productivity and zone of indifference?
>
> Is there one margin for both capital and labor? Or separate margins?
>
> Taussig can't reconcile Clark's zone of indifference and later theory of margin. In zone of indifference return only to labor; at margin, return both to labor and capital.
>
> At margin, determine rate of return to both. Therefore Taussig would throw over case of indifference.
>
> Marshall's reasoning looks like Clark's, only he adds "this isn't theory of wages".

Apr. 1

Writers agree that in static conditions that successive increments of capital don't bring equal returns.

> —— What becomes of this
> A B   when B is added

1. In case of land, difference goes as rent.
2. Applying diagram to theory of value (commodities) goes as consumers surplus.
3. Income of capital, Clark's idea that it goes as wages.

Difference between land and capital is fixity in amount of land.

Difference in serviceability to community of different capital goods of same pecuniary value.

Conclusion.

There is a sense in which there is a universal law of diminishing returns, both for land and capital: but it must be borne in mind that the successive units of capital are interchangeable, whereas land is fixed. In that sense a difference in returns from land and capital.

Apr. 4

Assignment

Taussig – Principles, Ch. 51, Paragraphs 4–9.
Fetter – Ec. Principles, Ch. 11–13.

Böhm-Bawerk – Criticism of Clark

(Taussig) Value of Clark's differentiation between capital and capital goods valuable in reducing the common denominator. In Ricardian phraseology, means common estimation of value. (Ricardo value equals quantity of labor.)

Böhm-Bawerk holds theory of internist as due to preferences for present over future. Productivity theory of capital. Impatient with begging-of-question in productivity theory. Thinks Clark relapses to this old productivity theory.

Two separate questions

1. Is there separable, specific product of capital?
2. If there is product imputed to capital, is it properly ascribable to capital?

    Böhm-Bawerk accuses Clark of presupposing a rate of interest, i.e., net returns to capital, and that it is specific product of capital.

Apr. 6

Assignment

Savers' Rent.
F.W.T. [Taussig] – Ch. 39.
Wolfe – *Q.J.E.* Nov. 1920[14]

Böhm-Bawerk Theory.

Return to current labor and tool is greater than return to what labor alone would get. This difference in return is not interest, but a globular sum which includes both interest and depreciation and in main is attributable to past labor. Thus joint return to current labor and tool is really return to present and past labor. Therefore no definite specific product of capital reasoning leads to circular reasoning – wages determined; by interest, interest determined by wages. Taussig says no specific product attributable to capital.

General Level of Wages.

Why difference in wages between countries?

U. S. higher than Great Britain
Italy higher than Greece
Before war Germany about like Great Britain

Wide range of wages in U.S. and G.B. both, but level is higher than U.S.
1. Clark would answer, due to greater specific product in U.S.
2. Ricardo might have said it was due to higher rate of wage, or that capital in U.S. was advancing faster than population.
3. Cairnes would any ratio of effective capital (i.e., fund available to wages) to laborers is higher in U.S.
4. Taussig – general wages determined by discounted [above "advance"] marginal [above "last"] product of labor. Therefore higher level in U.S. because higher discounted marginal product.

Concept of Marginal Product.

Is it same as Clark?

Clark would cut out theory of "zone of indifference" and leave essentials of reasoning unaffected.

In Clark's reasoning surplus produced over and above marginal product of labor is source of capital, i.e., concept of different degrees of productivity of labor (Taussig rejects zone of indifference).

Taussig assumes a competitive margin.

Different localities and establishments set level of wages.

Great difference in cost curve between different establishments, due to

different ability in management. Curve like this.

Apr. 6

Marginal Discounted Product.

Taussig differs from Clark. As far as distribution is concerned, no difference between employees in any one establishment. This needs qualification. For instance in big retail establishment, some – those on ground floor – are making more money than those on upper floors. This is basis of site rent. Always get more for ground floor. Effectiveness of labor on ground floor is source of rent to the establishment. Clark's zone of indifference indicates some laborers produce only wages therefore some laborers must produce more than wages else there would be no interest. Hard to reconcile this with other theory of marginal productivity determining wages.

Taussig says wages in one establishment same – differences come between firms, i.e., competitive margin.

Question of amount of super-marginal return. Davenport held biggest part.[15] Nobody knows.

What Determines Rate of Discount?

1. Established rate of time-preference – irksomeness of waiting?
   (Like Mill' tendency to a minimum).
2. Ricardian – blind impact of demand and supply. Ricardian in likeness to theory of balance of population and supply of capital. Natural rate of wages, and interest emerged as surplus.
3. Alternative – agnosticism as the rate of interest.
4. Keene [unidentified] – regulating the standard of living of Poles, Slavs, etc., i.e., unskilled labor in U.S. Keene later gave it up for agnosticism.

Applicability of conformation of supply curve.

If concept of steady increase with two determining factors, supply and demand, no telling where lines will meet, i.e.

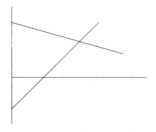

Wolfe uses results of Prof. Friday. Friday investigated inflowing accumulations and found large amount in form of profits put back into business. Shows in excess profits tax. Peculiarity of this form of savings is that it involves no weighing of present vs. future – corporation does saving therefore looks like blind impact.

Comments:

1. Business profits in U.S. take preponderantly the form of dividends, not lump sum as under older organization (Walker). Therefore Friday is calling attention to fact that great source of unflowing accumulation is business profits in form of dividence and corporation and surplus.

    Therefore question is what are motives which underlie this form of saving which forms so important a part of U.S. accumulations.

2. Necessary to distinguish between forces which make for original saving and for its retention or maintenance of capital.
    a. Clark says original capital once accumulated maintains itself. Question.
    b. Maintenance of accumulation may require interest.

Conclusions.

1. Guess rework as to conformation of supply curve always will be

2. Rate of interest has remained pretty steady since establishment of secure investment.

    Years in near future will probably see decline in rate.

Apr. 11

Assignment

Fetter – Ch. 14, 15, 20, 21, 22–25.
        Ch. 16, 18, 19.
Clark – Introduction and Ch. I.
        (and note his attitude toward ethical aspects of doctrine)

Fetter belongs to radical, original group of American economists which includes Fetter, Clark, Irving Fisher, Alvin S. Johnson.

Two fundamental sets of doctrines mark this set of writers:

1. Doctrine of specific, marginal productivity of capital
2. Denial validity of distinction between rent and interest – No good means for maintaining old differences between rent and interest. Curve goes part way with them agrees #1 but not #2.

Carver reviewed Clark, agreed with marginal productivity theory, and disagreed with synchronizing theory. Neither Clark nor Marshall face fact of inequality. Scientific attitude of Carver, Clark, Böhm-Bawerk to distribution is "unconscious humbug".

Fetter.

Rejects unscientific terminology of most economics. Therefore, tried experiments in development of technical vocabulary.

Fetter drops phrase utility – marginal, final, total as misleading and uses stratification.

Fetter's terminology

1. "Gratifications", instead of utility.

   Neutral term. (Fisher's "desirability") Cf. German wert equals value, but not value in exchange – more what philosophy calls value.

   Preis (price) according to Germans means more what Fetter means by price – i.e., in sense of exchange value in terms of anything else. (Usually used to denote money) Fetter's interpretation of price like Fisher.

2. Consumptive and durative uses, commodities why not consumable:

   Former used up in one operation.
   Latter used over and over again.

   This leads to consumptive and durative uses of commodities and then the consumptive and durative usances. "Uses equal physical yield or output of a thing (but not gratification in sense of psychic income). Use vs. horsepower of electric plant.

   Usances come about as near to quasi-rent as anything, i.e., net yield over and above expenses. A pecuniary concept.

Apr. 13

Assignment

Hobson: Work and Wealth
Consider carefully Fetter on Wages – Ch. 16, 18, 19.
Read Fetter – Ch. 26, 28, 29.

<u>Fetter</u>.

Reasoning in connection with controversy with Böhm-Bawerk. Two theories of interest

1. Productivity theory.
2. Time-preference theory.

Nassau set going theory of interest as reward for abstinence – little change till Clark formulated productivity theory: Böhm-Bawerk wrote about same time. Clark's theory a strong productivity; theory – interest is sharply demarcated product of capital. Theory accepted by Carver. Different from Bashat [unidentified; possible Bastiat].

Böhm-Bawerk set up time-preference theory, followed in fundamentally by Fetter, i.e., interest due to preference for present over future. In with this theory in Böhm-Bawerk is line of reasoning more in accord with productivity than time-preference idea, i.e., theory of effectiveness of roundabout method of production – use of tools which don't result in finished product for some time. Leads Böhm-Bawerk to theory that present labor yields product only in future therefore rejects Clark's theory of synchronization. Böhm-Bawerk describes <u>roundabout process</u> will – gathering materials, making tools, ultimately result in greater product.

Böhm-Bawerk goes further and lays down law of diminishing returns in than with roundabout process. Published main lines of reasoning Behaviorists in periodicals before publishing book. Says in applying roundabout process, first application of tools makes biggest increase of product; thereafter increase of product proceeds at a diminishing rate. Böhm-Bawerk lays this down as inevitable process. In later edition, works out theory of diminution of returns more fully. [In margin: "Behavorists would saw he 'followed his bent' like Ricardo"]

Böhm-Bawerk denies that this is productivity theory – its an illustration of way theory of time-preference works out. So works to conclusion; that <u>interest is perpetual</u> – may decrease but it will continue. Tausaig says it is "bringing in productivity theory by back door."

<u>Fetter</u> goes back to a more nearly pure time-preference theory. Goes with Clark in rejecting between interest and rent; but disagrees on productivity theory.

Fetter and Fisher agree. In roundabout process and its consequences, Fetter is awkward and obscure. Means to say time-preference dominates the roundabout process. The idea of Böhm-Bawerk that the more roundabout the process, the more effective it is, has nothing to it. Says Fetter, those methods of roundabout process will be adopted which are in accord with time-preference and also state of arts. Böhm-Bawerk puts it just the other way around i.e., roundabout processes determine time-preference. Fetter says time-preference determines rate of interest, given fixed rate of time-preference. Taussig thinks productivity theory is bound up by implication in Fetter. [In margin: "i.e. Rate of time-preference is at given time, fixed by outside conditions apart from productivity of capital."]

Fetter's Phraseology and Belated Problems.

Interest is term applicable only to monetary transaction of lending money, getting back more.

> Shouldn't say building yields interest – lump sum rent for usance not related to sum invested except as building is capitalizing equal parts basis.
>
> Fetter here applying same kind of reasoning as Marshall's quasi-rent. Every concrete instrument yields a rent.
>
> Renting contract equals contract involving usance of curative instrument. Fetter doesn't consider that as only thing which determines rate of return.
>
> Fetter said that when Marshall admitted quasi-rent he threw up the sponge – Marshall replied [blank] for long periods, below
>
> Read Taussig– concluding Chap. on Interest and Rent.
>
> Fundamental point of dispute about interest and rent hinges on freedom of Competition and equalization of rate of return on instruments. – Clarke Fetter, and Fisher don't see bearing on social question.
>
> (Consider application of usance doctrine to human services next time.)

Apr. 25

Assignment

Hobson: Work and Wealth – Ch. 3 and 4.

Doctrinal Relations Between Fetter and Fisher.

Same view as regards amalgamation of rent and interest notion – here both agree with Clark. Rent and interest different ways of looking at same thing. Same attitude toward problems of wages.

But in definition of interest different. Fetter confines it to contractual payment for sum of money – keeps to business terminology. Profits with Fetter as with accountant, doesn't include interest – profits is surplus on outgoings.

It is a reaction against excessive <u>normalizing</u>. Perhaps excessive <u>theorizing</u>. On building, Fetter sees <u>usance</u> and therefore not pure economic rent – Marshall calls it quasi-rent.

Fishers' theory of interest – sees interest as all-pervasive. A difference in terminology. Fisher means that the element which underlies all exchanges is <u>time-preference</u>. In buying house, Fetter says you buy <u>usance</u>; Fisher says interest enters through time-preference. Difference between Fetter and Fisher one of terminology – analysis and conclusions not unlike.

Fetter's Theory of Wages.

Fetter regards wages as analogous to rent in Fetterian sense of payment for usance value of capital goods. <u>Is labor a commodity</u>?

This is aleatory element in buying man's service; and labor is indefinitely extensible, but land is not. But these aren't fundamental.

Is payment for free labor like buying a slave or like buying a machine?

Apr. 7

<u>Assignment</u>

<u>Wages as Bent for Usance Value – Is Labor a Commodity</u>.

> Do wages depend on product, or product on wages?
>
> Does patent law and copyright law confirm Fisher's view?
>
> Neither Fetter nor Fisher consider the instinct of continuance, good workmanship. Fetter so bound up with application of rent and usance value that he fails to see he is dealing with an entirely different set of problems in dealing with labor.
>
> Question of rent and usance raises wider problems then is indicated by Fetter and Fisher. Raises question of non-competing groups. Psychological question of instinct of workmanship.
>
> Patent system rests on principle that it is necessary to bring out the desired product. <u>Is it necessary</u>? Patent system confirms Fetter and Fisher.
>
> Fetter and Fisher argue that product depends on reward.
>
> In this connection consider principle of rewards in proportion to
> 1. Service
> 2. Sacrifice
>
> Fundamental question

Hobson.

Idea of Income.

National dividend is net remainder of goods and services. Does not include wear and tear of labor, but does include wear and tear on tools and instruments, etc. This common idea – Hobson objects. Taussig says very different motives, in maintaining supply of instruments and supply of labor therefore he wouldn't agree with Hobson in deducting from dividend for wear and tear of labor.

Apr. 29

Assignment

Hobson – Ch. VII, Par. 5, 6, Ch. VIII.

National Income; Real Income – Costs and Utilities.

Net Utilities

   Hobson means different thing by utilities from Marshall or Fetter's "gratifica-tions," Fisher's satisfaction. Utilities equal net constituents of human happiness according to Hobson.

   Artists, inventors, etc., in whom creative faculty is strong incur no cost, and instead there is income involved for them in their activities therefore some activi-ties which involve no cost, and belong to gross national income.

   Business leaders – creative instinct, but must deduct for wear and tear, nervous energy. Also a certain callousness for businessman.

   Question where to strike balance.

   Callousness on increase for businessmen in dealings with immigrants. An [blank] characteristic. How far can you introduce such [blank] factors into eco-nomics? Economics seeks conclusions of a measurable sort.

   Hobson regards risk as a cost.

      Is risk a cost or utility? Doesn't business man enjoy the adventure?

      Carver says we are in dark as to the risk curve – some who enjoy it, others who do a lot of worrying. How about those in between? We don't know!

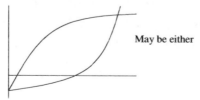

May be either

Monotony of Labor: Has Factory Increased it?

Marshall claims it has decreased monotony of labor – machine has taken over the repetitive processes. Ex. [blank], ditch digging, mine pumps.

Machine is unceasingly [blank]. Hobson says – tends to make worker automatic; must adapt himself to machine's pace.

Hobson points out mechanical character of machine tending. Taussig disagrees – weaver and spooler.

Munsterberg[16]: Psychology and Industrial Efficiency

Says many people like monotonous task.Some like it – others hate it!

Intermediate curve unknown.

Carver's theory applicable here also.

May 2

Hobson's summary of Net Utilities.

Much work is really costly in Hobson's sense. Attitude to work an important factor in determining human costs (Ex. Economics Prof. who curried horses in war). Hobson right in pointing out effect on interest in work and complex division of labor – worker separated from produce. Inevitable – also wage system in large scale industry.

Hobson's Analysis of Saving.

How compares with Clark's view that new capital only requires abstinence?

Hobson says new saving involves cost as well as maintenance. Therefore here Hobson conservative. Idea of uncertain future vs. certain present, and continuance of sacrifice so long as saver does without his property.

Differential sacrifice of savers – some incur much greater sacrifice.

Doctrine of saver's rent.

Hobson follows essentially conservative view in analysis of saving in idea of postponement, abstinence. Nothing fundamental different in saving by Shakers and modern capitalistic saving.

Hobson's analysis.

Saving by very rich – no human cost

Saving by middle class – some human cost – some economic cost.

Saving by very poor – very great human cost, with interest or not, therefore costless in economic sense of laying up for rainy day.

But Hobson doesn't deny economic cost for poor.

Orthodox analysis of very rich that saving yield large economic rent but do really involve some economic cost.

Hobson says no cost at all.

Hobson's analysis is as you go down scale, contains considerable divergence from orthodox analysis.

Interesting in that he has no quarrel with fundamental theory of saving.

Question if there isn't [blank] utility for very poor in saving (Taussig).

Perhaps Hobson goes too far in condemning thrift of very poor. Suppose socialistic state – Hobson would any increments might come costlessly from large national dividend – constant secretion of capital by unconscious process.

Assignment

Hobson – omit Ch. IX, X, XI.

May 4

Secretion of Capital in Well-Organized State and its Relation to Doctrine Of Human Cost.

In socialistic state, to get increase of productive power, the people would divide among themselves less than they might have had otherwise, i.e., adequate supply of costless capital – costless in human sense.

Hobson sees this costless secretion of capital to go back into production again therefore eventually increase in net human utilities. Starts argument with adequate provision for utilities and that therefore saving is costless and results only in increases of utilities. If this were the case, in order that there be increases in utilities, this presupposes change in standard of living in the meantime, also original saving couldn't be costless as Hobson says it was therefore only way out from Hobson's theory is on basis of change in standard of living.

Three Factors in Consumption.

1. Physical. – climate, environment – granted

2. Industrial –
   a. [blank] from worker may mean net loss in human utility
   b. injurious effects of sedentary life
3. Conventional

Some hold that entire absorption in one line of work bad therefore combine manual and mental work.

Conventional Factors.

Conventional factors in standard of consumption from lower classes.

From economic standpoint many things done by poor are wasteful which from human standpoint aren't – funerals, bank holidays.

Analysis of standards for others.

Importance of imitation. Things found to have human utility are imitated. Imitation leads to net loss of utilities. Theory of Leisure Class – ostentatious waste and conspicuous – leisure imitated by those who can't afford it. Veblen shows wrong of national waste.

Shows how propertical income come into being – book misnamed really theory of Manifestations of Leisure.

Conclusions.

Conspicuous waste not conducive to net human utility.

May 9

Sport, Culture and Charity.

Two lines

1. Co›k-fighting, professional baseball, bull-fishing.
2. Sporting life of well-to-do, imitation of it by poorer classes, and significance of intellectual dilettantism.

#1 Hobson's point of view leads to different discussion and treatment, from that of economist which is mainly quantitative. People who can bridge both fields rare.

Main thesis of chapter: sporting life, culture, charity are indulged in for their prestige value and are quite futile socially.

#2 Viewed as waste by Hobson. According to classical economists source of income is important.

(A. Smith: Capacity of human stomach is limited.
             Capacity of man for ostentatious satisfaction is unlimited.)

Unproductive Consumption equals that consumption which need not take place; part of income which man free to dispose of as he wishes. (Classical Economist view). This, according to them, is the bait for productive efficiency.

What can be considered waste?

cf. Hobson and classical economists.

May 11

Assignment

Hobson – Ch. XII.
        1. Sec. 1–8
        2. Sec. 9–15

Classical Economist's Analysis of Waste.

Waste equals direction of energy and consumption from which one gets nothing. So far as economist goes there is no waste. Senior says that even if means are indefinitely increased some satisfaction can be gotten from its use.

Behaviorists psychology would reason in terms in instinct of play and chase.

Waste a question of degree, i.e., ribbon worn by village lass and jewels of society leader.

Then discussion of waste resolves itself into a question of inequality, not that waste in itself is futile.

> Corollary to theory of diminishing returns that inequality of wealth doesn't make for maximum satisfaction. But quantitative measurement impossible.

Reason that classical economists failed to consider this; – they had considered emulation and imitation, but hadn't considered behaviorist arguments, i.e., how far, to secure maximum happiness, must there be free expression or repression of instincts with us. They were of hedonistic, pain and pleasure, school.

Orthodox argument in defense of inequalities is that there must be paid of large returns to secure the maximum production. (cf. Hobson's idea that men exercise their creative faculties for the joy of it). All part of same problem. Fisher ignores this.

Hobson on Intellectual Culture.

Greek, Latin, and conventional utility. "Finishing school" as cf. women's college typify intellectual futility. A good deal to it. Practical education.

Old school hedonistic; new school marginal.

Old school emphasizes need of bait; new school sees importance of creative instinct.

May 13

Human Law of Distribution.

Production		Consumption
Art and exercise	)- Human utility	-(Needs
Labor	)-	(Abundance
Toil	)- Human Cost	-(Satiety
Mal-production)		(Mal-consumption

Exercise equals pleasurable physical activity

Art equals pleasurable creative activity

Labor equals moderate amount of productive activity.

> Brings no pleasure to individual but yields net utility to society. Involves idea of interdependence of individuals – therefore good for individual as member of society to contribute therefore serviceable to society. [In margin: "See Hartley Withers' "Meaning of Money," "The Case for Capitalism"][17]

Toil equals excess of labor, which would bring net gain to society.

> Human cost involved is greater than productive gain and resulting utility to society.

Mal-production equals degrading work.

> Analysis leads to "from each according to his ability, to each according to his needs".

What Individualist Would Say.

1. Quarrel with distinction between labor and toil
2. No such thing as satiety, or practically none

Is Hobson objection to inequalities of wealth or to fact that labor has social solidarity and toil hasn't.

Individualist would say that both labor and toil has social solidarity. Ex. Household labor. Toil inevitable in system in which worker is urged to do his best.

Hobson's Scheme of Distribution.

> Distribution according to need.
>
> Modifications:
>
> 1. Difference of organic needs – some workers need more to eat.
> 2. Must consider productive efficiency. Differences not between classes but within class, i.e., better physicians.

May 16

Assignment

Hobson – Ch. XIII, XV

Individualism and Marginalism.

Laissez-faire polices, a line of action; individualism an analysis which leads to laissez-faire polity.

Individualism: Premise –

1. Individual left to follow his own interest will best serve interests of all.
2. Old school, with theory of equalizing differences in wages, unconsciously held to idea of perfect mobility of labor (cf. Cairnes' non-competing groups).
3. Older economists held theory, of maximum satisfactions accruing automatically in letting men pursue their own interests unfettered – this underlain by idea that "covetousness is held in check by covetousness," i.e., freedom of movement.

   No freedom of movement between labor and capital, Taussig says.

Premises of Marginalism (Hobson)

1. Infinite divisibility of factors of production.
2. Mobility of labor and capital (in order to get idea of equality and of return at margin)

Does Marginalistic analysis apply one formula to labor and capital?

Marginalists differ – Carver makes differential element applicable in regard to capital goods; different from marginalistic idea applicable to labor with differential element.

Clark applies it to both.
Hobson is attacking Clarkian School.

Therefore, premises of marginalistic doctrine different.

Given supply of instrument of production, reward determined by marginal install-ment of supply.

Therefore, marginaliam adjusted to non-competing groups – individualism not for it held permanent differences could be ironed out. Cairnes' didn't know how much he was giving up in accepting non-competing group[s].

Marginalism an analysis: a doctrine without a slant; in no sense a justification of things as they are. Often given a slant, as in Clark, who implies that it is right that everyone get the marginal contributions of his class.

[In margin: "See May Q.J.E., Adams on Excess Profits Tax"]

Adams concludes in Excess Profits' Tax that U.S. Government not clever enough to handle it; same argument for individualist on land tax – last defense vs. such tax; argument vs. inheritance tax that state will spend – thus breaking up capital to spend it. (Hence suggestion that State never be allowed to spend money from inheritance tax).

May 20

Assignment

Hobson – Ch. 16, 19

> Robson on Marginalism.
>
> Defect in that it assumes that market value measures worth, and that everyone gets what he is worth.
>
> Marginalist mechanism same when applied to labor as to capital or dif-ferent groups of labor.
>
> Analogous case – Austrian School reasoned similarly to get value of commodities – value determined by marginal utility.
>
> Is it circular reasoning? – thing receives what it is worth, and it is worth what it receives.

Contribution of last man in group determines reward of group. This isn't to say a man gets what he is worth – but what he is worth is determined by contribution of last man in a group.

Taussig says specific productivity theory not essential part of marginalism. Marginal stands without it.

Hobson says also that marginalism

1. Assumes infinite divisibility of factors of production.
2. Perfect mobility of labor and capital.

This is just criticism of marginalism of Clark, but it doesn't mean general theory. He has justificatory slant but this isn't necessary to marginalism. Hobson says, too, it ignores surplus – true of Clark who smoothes out <u>rent</u>, but ordinary marginalism doesn't. Marginalism may lead to recognition of producer's and consumer's surplus. Therefore Hobson's criticism of ordinary marginalism incorrect.

<u>Piece Work vs. Salary</u>.

Salary system is one week. Eliminated, disregards irregularity of employment, gives security of employment.

Essence of piece work is paying men according to what they do, not on basis of a man doing his best.

Both systems attempt to reward in proportion to contribution.

No man knows what is in him till he tries. So between strong and weak man. Theory that people spontaneously exercise their powers independent of reward probably an exaggeration. Piece work a practical expression of dissent from this view – <u>how far is material reward necessary</u>? Anyway Hobson doesn't bring out psychological question involved. Assumes everyone will do his best spontaneously. Other extreme is to say only external stimulus is to get reward in proportion to effort.

Consider Hobson's Constructive Proposals.

May 23

<u>Hobson's Positive Scheme of Reconstruction.</u>

1. Distribution on basis of needs, with bonus, a bribe, to those whose faculties are especially worth stimulating.
2. Division between public and private control of industries
   a. Routine industries under public control
   b. Creative industries under private control
      What are they? Two possible bases for discrimination
      Routine
      1. Emergence of monopoly (Marx)

    2. Standardization of processes, settling down. Fairly routine conduct (Hobson)

Ex. Hydro-electric power, for getting electricity at mines though monopoly is on the horizon Hobson would leave under private controls.

Therefore Hobson wants creative industries, whether in monopoly or competitive stage under private control. Reason for this is value of creative activities and abilities. Creative ability and activity an element of cost.

Hobson concedes this as Webbs do rent of ability to surgeon, though perhaps they only allow less than he would get under free competition.

Taussig says maturity and monopoly characteristic of public service industry. Hobson says only maturity.

  3. To what extent will private property exist.
    a. Will allow consumer's capital, but with better distribution.
    b. Hobson doesn't want sudden expropriation; but with Webbs and Fabians wants gradual expropriation with compensation, but even this compensation will be gradually taken over by State via inheritance tax. Inheritance tax plays important part in Fabian scheme.

[In margin: "?"] Public control of routine industries inevitable under Hobson's scheme. Doesn't make it clear about creative industries. probably doesn't contemplate interest's ceasing – a considerable body of interest; but has Regniano's [unidentified] theory of state as borrower and lender. Will get money via inheritance tax, taking 1/3 with each generation. Complicated book-keeping.

  4. Salary basis of payment, largely on basis of needs. Therefore an adjustment.
  5. Fundamental necessity for Hobson's scheme is cooperation – "an effective social will."

Hobson faces fact of inefficiency of public officials – has very definite doubt. (cf. Cole's convictions regarding man's creative instincts). Hobson open-minded in facing problem.

May 27

Hobson's Scheme of Reconstruction (Cost)

  1. Routine industries under state control
  2. New enterprises under private control

Wagner's *Katheder–Sozialismus*[18]
    Social insurance.
    State control of limited range of industries.
    Railroads, gas, street railways, i.e., public utilities.
3. Is Hobson inconsistent in condemning Wagner's program and advocating a wider range of industries under State. Webbs says that control of public utilities by state is consumer's cooperation.
State socialism is destined and designed to take care of consumers; and Hobson objects to control which represents only consumer. Hobson there quite consistent in condemning State Socialism and advocating his own scheme.
4. He objects to Syndicalism because it neglects the consumer.
5. In his routine industries, to take place of incentive, there must be effective social will, i.e., cooperation and cooperation of labor.
    (Division of labor is the unconscious cooperation of labor.) Therefore Hobson says one must develop the social point of view – altruism.

Is this distinction between creative and routine industries, latter requiring social point of view valid; whereas in creative industries extra bribe is necessary?
    Perhaps he has things wrong end to – bribe more necessary in routine industries.
If you get effective social will you don't need special reward in creative industries – perhaps even less needed here for there is play of spontaneity.
Social will more easily developed in creative industries.
Two reasons for difference in marginal effectiveness of men:
    1. More, better inborn qualities
    2. More assiduous, try harder
       In routine industries depends on #2
       In Creative industries depends on #1

For which do you need greater reward?

Hobson more fair-minded when he allows for difference in opinion on this – nobody knows.
[In margin: "Read Ch. 20 Hobson"] Hobson speaks of Direct Social Will and Organic Concept of Society. Says direst social will means effective [blank], works to direct individual will.
Sociological doctrine of social will.
McDougall: Group Mind.
Analogy of social and biological organism.
Taussig question group mind, social will.

June 1

Future of Economic Science.

Course has been a series of exercises in the "Grand Style." Austrian School and American followers, Clark, Fetter, and Fisher belong to class of "grand style." But don't point the way to further progress.

Two most promising leads:
1. Statistical method and its adaptation to economic science.
   Here include historical approach.
2. Social, behaviorist psychology.

Statistical Observation.

More material available – figures, data. Refinement of statistical method.
  Ex. 1. Possibility of cost curves. Significance of their conformation.
  Ex. 2. Source of savings.
  Ex. 3. Business cycles.

Economist must be content with slow accumulation of facts on which to base theories. Combination of analysis, hypothesis, always in readiness for new leads.

Possibility of application of statistical method to question of social stratification and differences in ability. Subject overlooked in economics and sociology.

Hammond's books on Eng. Agricultural Laborer suffer from fact that they start with a slant and looking for proof. Same with Havelock Ellis only here less of slant.[19]

Social psychology.

Possibilities in analysis of motives. Some objections – Carver says motives don't matter. Böhm-Bawerk says interest in psychology of value – but why people value things not in field of economics. Criticism just if economics is Taxonomic science; not if its a genetic science. As taxonomic science, subject of economics is analysis of things as they are; as genetic science, how they come to be.

Can there be quantitative movement?
  How know extent of altruism?
  How know extent of selfishness?

SUPPLEMENTAL NOTES FROM F.W. TAUSSIG'S COURSE IN ECONOMIC THEORY WITH CONTRIBUTIONS BY A.A. YOUNG

ECONOMICS 11
(SUPPLEMENTARY NOTES)
PROFESSORS TAUSSIG AND YOUNG.
1921–1922

MAURICE B. HEXTER

ECONOMICS 11

H. George, Progress & Poverty – Book I	Walker-Discussion
P.A. Walker, Wages Question, Ch. VIII, IX	I-359–I-383
P.A. Walker, Pol. Economy, Part IV, Ch. 5, 6	Walker-Pol. Ecno.
(Adv. Course) Part VI, No. 5	Part IV. Ch. IV.

1870 Mill at height of prestige at publication and George and attached the principle that wages paid out of capital. It was a pretty well marshaled attacked (not systematic).

Thought I	George says source of wages was product
Page 59	Labor according to George produces more than before he is paid.
	George really means rendering of value before he gets value received.
	Mill would reply that only one kind of capital was used for the advance– i.e. circulating capital.
II	The case of idler only brings in question of distribution.
Page 73–75	Close analysis shows most part of production is upon last labor. Even here, most of the articles were produced by past labor.
III	(Get quotation)
Page 75	Marshall said wages-fund theory neglected personal qualities of the worker.
IV	Case of isolated Englishmen and Africans on island with years. Years supply is past product and, therefore, capital.
	Walker would say that with greater production of Englishmen the wages would be higher than Negroes.
V	See Note 1 (p. 134) Laborer advances to capitalist. Example of street railroad. Walker here considers the source of wages.
	Different meaning of product used by Walker than in case IV.

In one case it is a tangible thing.

(Note difference between source of and method of payment of wages)

And in other case (V) he means service. Mix-up comes in payment of wages in cash, value, or goods. Shifting point of view and apply to second case the finding of first.

From Smith to Walker, this shifting occurred.

For our purpose we must decide between money wages and real wages.

Real wages for us more important. Must have clear distribution between capital and whose capital (and product and whose product).

Advancement of wages by capital and payment of wages in kind are two very different things.

VI   Case of partial advance – American farmer who provides board and advance money for.

This payment of money is not a payment out of product because their product was only of one specific kind. Contemporary labor puts finishing touches to the consumable goods. George said labor paid out of contemporaneous labor. [Note in margin: "Ricardo, Principle of Pol. Econ."]

(Date of turnover – refers only to last stage of the process)

Taussig: The product we now use is part product of labor. Must distinguish between the product and the money wage. The wages fund should be called a flow. [Blank] not in mind of the "old" men. The flow is determined by the condition of the past. There is a certain placement of predetermination.

Wages flow should be called Income flow because all get their subsistence from it. Came about because of difference between goods consumed by laborer and rich.

I.

Cap.	Prod.	Profits	Corn		Cap.	Prod.	Profits	Rent
	16-2/3%					75%		
60	100	10	30		60	125	45	20
60	90	10	20		60	115	45	10
60	80	10	10		60	105	45	
60	70	10	–					

	58-1/3%		
60	125	35	30
60	115	35	20
60	105	35	10
60	95	35	

This shows extreme variations of profits Which he says in first charter an value does not vary much.

Here profits go up to 75% where only three sections farmed by reason of increasing productivity.

(Varying Amount of Land)

II.

Cap.	Prod.	Profits	Rent
		25%	
50	100	12.5	37.5
60	100	15	25
70	100	17.5	12.5
80	100	20	–

		33%	
45	100	15	40
55	100	18-1/3	26-2/3
65	100	21-2/3	16-1/3
75	100	25	

Different amount of capital necessary to farm the same land and get same product. But here he makes arithmetical mistake by dropping 5 points in each grade of diminution instead of proportionate reduction.

Individual capitalists have nothing to do with controlling the wages fund.

Theory of Distribution: Walker's development after onslaught on wages fund. Written on instigation of *Quarterly Journal of Economics* – See Walker's Pol. Econ. "Distribution"

Case Stated.

Dismisses subject of interest summarily that it is determined by supply and demand and reward for abstinence, although this was similar to theory regarding wages fund.

Rent accepts Ricardian theory.

Profits (independent share in distribution and Walker broke new ground. Hitherto they had meant something like wages and interest together.

Older ones has put double interest (Mill, Ricardo, Smith) all thought of profiles as essentially like interest. In this he contributes to distinctly American economics. Amount depended on ability of man and not on quantity of capital at your command.

Wages gets what is left. A residual process. [Note in margin: "Ricardo, Pol. Econ., Ch. 1"].

His theory had two elements:
1. Explanation of business profits.
2. New theory of amount paid as wages – has nothing to do with the source of payment.

Walker's conception of no-profits man

Difference between what poorest man gets and what each individual might get.

Walker seems to incline to day laborer's pay as basis of no-profits man.

Taussig's interpretation.

Walker had in mind the sort of job which is most readily open to the man who is making no profits – either manager or sub-manager. Small business people (e.g., main roads) not making profits and personnel continually shifts.

High salaries Walker would call "commuted" profits, although this man may be able to make more in his own business. He is not a no-profits man, as he may not be of adventurous spirit. This man was never explained by older economists.

Implication is that these profits not charge on product and does not take away wages. (Explained inequalities)

Development of Walker's Doctrine

No-profits man. (false employers) The small unsuccessful shopkeeper. Profits doctrine is no part of cost of production of that cost of production which determined price; i.e., high business profit no deduction from wages. They get what they produce.

[In margin: "According to Taussig"] Suppose Walker is right that profits and wages come out of present product, he really argues in circle because he says wages are what is left after all is taken and then profits are what are left after wages are deducted.

(Walker uses term "no-profits" which we call wages by interpretation)

(But Walker might have said "I mean by wages 'the whole globular mass of wages'".) And two meanings to wages and "no-profits" are not wages.

Walker had a cheerful view of wages and could not mean subsist wages and said wages determined by productivity.

Mill – Bk. III, Ch. XV on Measure of Value.

Ricardo:

Chap. I contains controversial matter. Value is amount of labor an article would common, and also value determined by amount of labor necessary to produce it.

Taussig says no absolute measure of value. Ricardo says value determined by amount of labor taken to produce.

Of. This with Henry George

George deals with source of distribution and Ricardo with determination of amount.

Mill – Bk. III, Ch.4

Essays – early dissenters against Mill
   T.E. Cliff – Leslie – Principle F. of theory of R. on value, depends on comparative quantity of labor.

Fundamental Assumption
a. Natural in savage times: minor premise
b. Natural in later society too: major premise

Minor premise: Fallacy of undistributed middle (no right to say that later like earlier.)

He would reply that people know in general way the amount of labor necessary to produce article, labor includes implements, etc. (see pp.16, 17).

Ricardo knew of the complexity, but we must admit that to determine amount of labor involved difficult if not impossible.

Also, labor to Ricardo was homogenous.

Important to know what occurs when travelling from simple to complex. But you must go step by step. Ricardo attempts this gradation by considering the difference.

Two sources of complication:
1. Different values of labor, competition, interchange and mobility – and complication when passing to complex society to know labor cost (See Section II). Important for Ricardo's theory involves that

all kinds of labor equal. There is difficulty in reconciling this view with his original statement. Ricardo would say ease, honorific facts of employment, bear on wages, but that this means amount of labor – (exertion) [In margin: "Ricardo, Ch. II; Mill, Bk. III, Ch. V."]

Ricardo accepted trend of his age. All men born equal. [In margin: "Of Mill, Bk. IV, Ch. III"]

Ricardo was interested in varying exchange rates in commodities.

Ricardo

100 laborers	100 = 10,000
With profits	20% = 12,000 – Ricardo would say
	10% 11,000

Relation between wages and profits increase according to Ricardo. But there is range in variability of profits with connoted corresponding variability of wages. There were mere changes in distribution due to changing money value.

****

110 @100	= 10,000 wages
Profits 10%	= 1,000
	11,000 price of commodity

50 men @ 100	= 5,000 making machines × 10% = 5,550
50 men @ 100	= 5,000 using machines × 10% = 5,550
	11,550

Define to physical capital in machine, which is used after finishing by ran for one year.

Ricardo said "the way in which wages are pd. (in this case spread over longer time) effects value"

Ricardo would say historically, profit did not vary greatly.

Ricardo assumed free completion of capital.

Ricardo assumed variation of rates of wages to be smaller insignificant.

Marx said Ricardo saw value equal to labor. Ricardian has only superficial similarity to Marxian. Ricardo had pure scientific spirit. Marx interested in proletariat and interested in showing capitalist takes surplus value. Must distinguish between pure and actual distribution of product. Assuming stability of money, any change in price resisters different amount of labor bestowed upon it. Values cannot be totaled – prices can be totaled (Ricardo somewhere speaks of adding to sum total of values, but number of valuable things can be increased).

Qualifications in Ricardian doctrine

1. Differential in labor – (we think very important for us)
2. Length of time over which labor is spread (not so important for us)

For his definition of rent, see p. 56; Ricardo introduced the differential element into rent and so to Ricardo the price of grain depends upon labor devoted to it and the price of grain on marginal land. This modifies the theory of value. Existence of rent proved that productivity was hard not easy. Price depends on quantity of labor devoted under most unfavorable circumstance. Those especially circumstanced get a differential. Rent is result of price and not cause of it. [In margin: "Ricardo, Ch. V"]

Effects of improvement upon rent
Rent of mined different proposition. There is no original and indestructible [four indecipherable words]. Forests are like mines and rent here is royalty, if it's a natural forest. Where forest it ran made there is a real rent. (Marshall said payment for land is always rent.) [In margin: "Einaudi: *La Reuditamin Eratia*"]

Relation between Mill and Ricardo.
Mil elaborates

Ricardo on Natural and Market Price: Started by Smith and fixed by Ricardo.

Ricardo implies that all tools, food and clothing comprise part of previous labor. He means by "capital" what the later ones mean by wages fund. Process was gradually so that everything was cropped by English Economists so that capital wages was only food. This was started by Ricardo. See p. 82. [In margin: "Did Ricardo believe in iron law of subsistence?"]

a. Means law of diminishing returns (wages rise)
b. Believed that standard of living was not absolutely fixed. Some part of his standard could be temporarily lowered.

Ricardo – Ch. VI &III
Mill – Bk. I, Ch. X, XI, XII, XIII
  Bk. II, Ch. I
  Bk. II, Ch. XI, XV
  Bk. IV, Ch. IV, V, VII

On Profits: Profits was skin to interest and payment for investments of capital. Rate is connected with interest. It was something more than interest, but varied with it.

> Ricardo had in mind (Taussig) that money wages might go up, as population increases and law of diminishing returns became effective, but laborer would be not so well off, as they don't go up so high.

> (In this chapter on taxes, Ricardo says the laborer would not pay tax as he would get more wages, otherwise he could not exist.) His problems also not hypothetical.

> Ricardo felt that corn wages never varied much, and that wages were fixed and money wages adjusted themselves quickly, but he assumes [indecipherable] of standard of corn necessities. Ricardo did believe in iron law.

Rate of profits fall, as population pressure fall:
  a. Money value of capital less
  b. More money capital investment needed

And so rate falls (Branliew [unidentified] same and also H.C. Carey), the result of which is that distribution becomes more equal.

 "Are poor getting poorer and rich getting richer?"

> Ricardo pointed tendency of profits to fall. Conceivable that rates decline but the aggregate increase. But eventually fall in rate will outweigh increase in aggregate.

> Source of increase of capital was from rent and profits and laborer never had anything.

> Landlord sole beneficiaries of social progress. Rent keeps on increasing and profits continue to fall. Landlords gain all.

> Figures cannot show whether rents rise, profits fall, or aggregate increase or decrease because he assumed poorer land taken in a fixed proportion and this is wrong assumption.

> ("If all land equally fertile and all land equally distant from market, would there be Rent?")

Effects of improvement in the arts on profits:

> According to Ricardo, is to stave off decline in profits or at times to raise them.

> Effect of improvement on price of commodity is quick. But when he applies reasoning to prices of agricultural commodities, wages will fall – iron law. As food becomes dearer, the wages go up, but not quite so much. Reducing price of goods consume by capitalists profits do not fall and so capitalists with same rate of profits is better off; the gain here is as consumer not as producer.

> Improvements in arts show slow effect and initial effect is to rains profits first and as other put them in the rates fall.

> Ricardo assumed immediate effectiveness. Eventually consumers benefitted. This process goes on repeatedly not only in one improvement but in all improvements. It is the succession of improvement which is important. The interval is important.

Ricardo – 1772–1823

1811	Letters on Price of Bullion
	Reply to Bosanquet
1815	Essay on Influence of low price of corn etc and low profits of stock
1816	Proposals for an economic and secure currency
1817	Principles (3rd edition, 1821)

In Parliament 1819–1823

1. Letters to Malthus, 1887
2. Letters to McCulloch, 1895
3. Letters to Trower, 1899

Ricardo became Christian by marriage. Identified with Englishmen of his time. Business at 20 and retired at 25. (Pitt's financial are height) then live intellectual life. First interest in natural science (geology). At 27 read Smith's Wealth of Nations, accidentally. Not interested in historical and statistical passages.

First appearance as writer was in 1809 on Market Price of Bullion (Bank of England had closed) to show high gold prices due to depreciation of bake notes. Let to reply Bosanquet.

> In 1815 published (see   )
> In 1817 published (see   ) [As in original]

In autobiography of J.S. Mill, we get idea how principles were written.

1816 see – later carried thru by feel in 1844

Also had proposal for National Bank – published after death 1824
1. To Malthus: Discovered by Bonar
2. See
3.

[As in original]

1819 – Entered Parliament by buying seat in [a] rotten borough and was active member. Very few honest men there and most of them orthodox. Ricardo was radical. Believe in parliamentary reform and appealed to current [missing words] his economic principles (see Cannan on life in parliament). Opposed prosecutions for blasphemy and opposed Wilber Force. Joined and then withdrew from an Owenite experiment. Believe in paying off national debt by capital levy.

History of his doctrine of value. It has two sources:

1. Adam Smith's doctrine of value (labor a commodity demanded or exchanged for)
2. Discussion from 1814–1817 going on in England on handling for national debt. This was handled or supposition of falling price of corn and consequent fall in money wages and hence fall in price of commodities. This influence review.

McCullough reason – grain goes down and money wages go down and all prices go down. Suggested reduction in interest rate in accordance with fall in price of corn, to equalize return.

McCullough out Ricardo

Ricardo said distinguish between general fall and fall of certain commodities.

What is left of his theory?

Ricardo thought labor all remains in same condition though money wages rise. Ricardo reasoned in precise terms and said with progress of society (unless there are improvements) profits fall, and landlord gets more and more. Cornerstone is determination of wage by price of food. This is Malthusian conviction and his own rent. Reasoned from premises that are not true that laborers will not work except on certain standard. Thought that after he had so reasoned that was all that had to be done.

Ricardo Bullion was best he did. Also the 1815 one is thorough and original and remarkable intellectual performance. [In margin: "Mill, Bk. II, Ch. XI"]

Quantity Fertilizer	Field	
	Grain	Straw
0.0	5.8	9.3
2.5	10.4	16.2
5.0	15.5	20.5
7.5	17.9	21.2
10	21.7	23.9
15	17.8	24.7
20	16.2	22.2

[In margin: "Esslen, Gesetz de Abrienhenenden Bodenertages"]

Mill:

1. Law of increase of labor
2. Law of accumulation of capital "effective desire for accumulation"

   This brings in personal element, as future must be visualized.

   Most of this is human institution and no physical law.

3. Law of increase of production from land. (Law of diminishing returns)

   Additional increment of labor returns a diminishing proportionate return and then you reach a maximum where additional units make no addition.

[In margin: "Mill, Bk, II, Ch. XV, with Ricardo"]

Mill on Wages.

By labor Mill means those who work for hire. This leaves out some groups. Arises from industrial change in England making large classes of agricultural laborers.

By capital he means that which is expended in direct purchases of labor. Does not get you very far. This is different use of word capital than he previously used.

(Ricardo makes same error, first talking tools, material and food and then the first two drop out). [In margin: "Get Taussig Wages & Capital"]

Wages-fund doctrine starts with Adam Smith. It was accepted by Mill at all because it fitted well with Malthusian[ism] and easily

Doctrine of this relationship not accepted now and Malthusianism is not fully accepted, although it cannot be wholly overthrown. Standards of living do rise and have risen. Birth rates do adjust themselves to standard of living. Laborer does not fully swallow up increase by more children.

Ricardo said wages depend directly on price of necessary food.

Mill said Ricardo assumed universal minimum wage rate.

Mill is wrong and is again due to Malthusianism pessimism. Mill tries to make Ricardo more scientific but Ricardo did not have these notions at all.

According to Mill profits include interest, insurance and wages of superintendence. Ricardo had said that there was a flat level of profile in all lines. This he had found somewhat in but not so ironclad. Mill said while individual make different profits the whole industry tends to equalize with all others (except monopolies). This separation of individual differences in wages of superintendence might lead to a separation of these three items and make of it a separate share, like Walker. After Mill this was forgotten and profits in same thing as interest as it was in Ricardo.

See statement p. 416 the cause of profits, etc. is Ricardian and is found in Ricardian discussion of value.

Profit emerges as surplus and is found in Ricardo. The second is the Marxian doctrine of mechanism of distribution and is also found in Böhm-Bawerk. Operation of capitalists consists of succession of advances to labor.

Mill (see p. 419) "We thus arrive...." See the three variables on p. 430. Wages to Ricardo defended upon labor spent in its production. (There are really only two variables: Efficiency of labor and reward of labor (Taussig).)

Ricardo had said that profits depend on price of food as labor gets a minimum.

J.S. Mill 1806–1873

East India Co., 1823–1828

1829	Essay on some unsettled question of Political Economy
1843	Logic

1848   Political Economy

1865–1868   Parliament

[In margin: "Note in text reading productivity theory of labor" and "Marshall, Bk. III, Ch. II, III, IV, VI"]

Son of James Mill who was in the radical group in first quarter of century. Friend of Ricardo and Bentham, Best known as father of his son. Wrote in the 1820s a book on Principle of Political Economy. [In margin: "Wicksteed – Common Sense and Pol. Econ. Bk. II, Ch. III"]

Wrote a history of British India.

Mill put through rigorous training by rather. In 1820–1821 lived in France with economist Say and had contact with French writers, St. Simonian School, the natural theory of progress. Knew Groat, the historian of Greece. Earlier, he contributed to Westminster Review. In 1829 published [blank in original]. In 1843 he published his System of Logic, his 6th Book, for discussion of method of social science. Political Economy published in 1848 and become ruling book. Married in 1851. Wages fund reunited by Mill after Thornton's book. 1851 he went to parliament for three years. Advocated extreme legislation and commanded respect, but did not affect course of legislation. [In margin: "A. Hobson, Work and Wealth, Ch. 22, pp. 320 – 337"]

The principle is a mosaic – made of pieces of all sorts of sources. Some from Smith. Most of the reasoning is from Ricardo. Sections from Rae, Senior, Wakefield, etc. The mosaic is well put together. There were two streams; Ricardo, value, capital. [In margin: "See Ch. V, Bk. I"]

In Ricardo wages fixed and profits variable. Mill saw progress meant accumulation of capital which could help laborers, see his static state chapter. Mill did not see the divergence. Mill never compared the different sections.

Marshall – Bk. III, Ch. 2, 3, 4, 5.

Use of term utility

> Swiss professor suggest other term which did not have dubious meaning of usefulness.

> Gratifications – Fetter

> Desirations – Fisher

Jevons brought it into English economics. Utility seems to hold its place.

Law of satiable wants and law of diminishing utility.

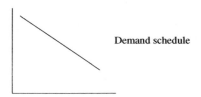

Demand schedule

While there are exceptions, they are unimportant, in the larger considerations. (e.g., Tastes change)

But other causes should pause us, e.g., music (Brahms).

The taste does not charge but a repetition brings a greater enjoyment.

But we accept the principle of diminishing utility, satiable wants, negative inclination of demand schedule.

What is meant by <u>demand:</u> Increase of demand and means shifting to right and upward and means quantity demanded is larger and also that same quantity can be sold at higher price. But shape of the curves need to be parallel but may be different.

Increase of <u>demand for money:</u> we use it somewhat differently than in talking of demand for commodities. Steeply inclined demand curve shows inelastic demand. (In a "rectangular hyperbola" the amount spent is constant or elasticity of demand is unity.)

This is the <u>strict</u> quantity theory of money. When quantity of money increases prices rise. <u>If demand for printing has been stimulated,</u> you mean elasticity of demand is greater than unity.

Fisher says "increase of demand" may be used in two senses:

a. In schedule sense that curve has shifted to right
b. In the market sense, demand has increase when merely negatively increased.

Economist sense is <u>a</u>.

There is a third sense.

a. Elasticity of demand. Total amount offered for the new price is greater than the old price.

Consumers Surplus:

That amount which a man gets by reason of the condition of the market.

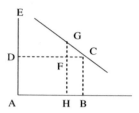

Some people get more out of a given good than others. That is consumer surplus, where supply is fixed.

It is an endeavor to get at measure of income in different terms, instead of money and goods. This attempts to put income in terms of satisfaction. Is there a possibility of measuring psychological income. This is what consumer surplus attempts to do.

Is there more to this theory when community made up of different strata than of one. This should probably not make much difference in continuity or discontinuity of demand.

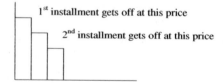

The demand schedule would still be continuous. Since the Jevons "price measures the marginal utility of an object, objected to because a poor man who buys the last object does not buy at higher prices because he cannot, not because the utility is less. Jevons assumed equality of income. Difficulty obviated by changing utility to marginal vendability (usefulness and ability). Utility means that unconsciously you neglect difference in income. If all incomes equal then man who pays high price has greater use and enjoyment. But difference arises when we have different strata. Marshall also says this. [In margin there is a line indicating the entire paragraph with the statement: "Marshall would admit this"].

Difference between necessities and non-necessities

In necessities consumers surplus is very great and we would better drop consumers surplus for to measure gratifications of necessities is gratuitous.

Pattern would call this a pain economy and consumer surplus does not work. This is another qualification.

Another qualification

Luxuries, e.g., diamonds. To apply the doctrine of consumer surplus we must state that the first purchase gets more gratification than later purchasers, but diamonds do not, as desire for distinction plays a great part.

So doctrine fails here, too, namely on articles used for purposes of distinction.

What's left?

Consumers surplus is excess of market yield and is like produces surplus or as Marshall called it earlier, consumers rent, like Ricardian rent doctrine. (Value of money is increase to its quantity – Ricardian an theory of money – see Taussig last chapter in Book on money, in his principles.) [In margin: "Mill, Bk. III, Ch. II. Marshall, Bk. V, Ch. I and II."]

School of Consumers Surplus

1. Can't say anything about it quantitatively, there is possibility of qualitative statement. Questions whether one suit is more valuable than another.
2. There is a marginal utility which is different from total utility – ("this is dirt cheap") Quantitative stamen possible.

Three senses

Increase of demand in schedule sense

Increase of demand in market sense

Increase of demand in elasticity

How would man enjoy A^1 and A^2

Communistic State would not deal with things about which consumers surplus would evaporate, e.g., diamonds.

Water one of comforts of life. But summer water does not satisfy any more than winter water.

(Deluxe editions and number edited sets is an attempt to cash in consumers surplus.)

Law of Supply and Demand

Mill means by demand the quantity demanded; it is an equation.

Marshall means an equilibrium price which means same thing.

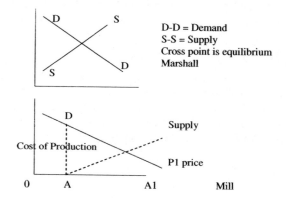

Mill's point is same as Ricardo & Smith, i.e., supply and demand.

Marshall said supply is not fixed and variations are not representative.

Cost of production:

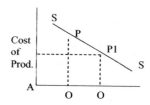

[In margin: "Mill, Bk. III, Ch. III; F.W. Taussig, Q.J. Econ. May 1921; Marshall, Bk. V, Ch. III, Ch. IV, Sec. 5, 6"]

> Mill said potential increase in supply would bring down price. Mill had in mind a flexible supply and bargaining between middlemen and not between consumers.
>
> Mill and Marshall ignore difference between middlemen dealing and the delivery to ultimate consumer.
>
> Market price for Mill and Marshall are those which we quote or prices between dealers. This modifies reasoning.

Price and maintenances.

Two conditions demand curve positively inclined.

a. Introduction of new element of gratification (Cadillac raising prices) with reference to ultimate consumers.
b. A threatened high price among transaction of dealers.

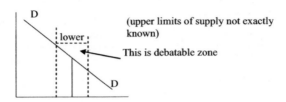

Mill's supposition of <u>fixed supply</u> has to be modified from the sharp statement of it like all Ricardian doctrines; e.g., cotton crop is now world crop.

Within the debatable zone, or penumbra, you can conceive a demand curve ⌣⌢ – sometimes negatively inclined and sometimes positive inclination. This would indicate diagrammatic exposition of more than one point of equilibrium. This would make market price indeterminate as supply curve also varies in its inclination.

Where a well-known operator unloads and others follow, we might think of demand curve as shifting left but this is result of fall in price. The demand curve within penumbra is demand curve dealers and outside penumbra it is demand curve of consumers and determined by utility. There is no one equilibrium but many of them. Utility of dealers not same as utility curves for consumers.

Marshall means by real cost of production.

Ricardo meant labor cost – on this deviated from Malthus.

Cairnes included abstinence which paid labor.

Malthus said must include wages or rather the interested necessary to get the money to pay the wages.

Marshall earlier divided expenses of production and cost of product (latter was real cost) former he drops and talks of cost.

"Representative firm is better off than no-profits man.

Mill wound not have called "market price" a normal price.

Marshall said market price is normal for the day.

Normal always relative to time taken. Normal price also for a season and normal long-period price (older fellows called this natural price) and normal price over generation or secular normal price (akin to Ricardo and Malthus period of falling wages or rising wages to subsistence).

Third conception of cf. this with Mill or [blank in original] is most important.

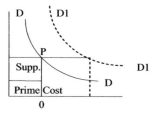

Prime cost – vary in proportion to output
Supplementary (overhead)

When demand suddenly shifts supply curve attempts to meet the demand curve and until it does there is larger than normal profit. But normally the demand curve shifts gradually. And so supply accommodates itself gradually. Divergence from the supply price from secular equilibrium is contingent upon suddenness of shifting demand. [In margin: "Agri. Rent Ch. C., Ch. VIII, Sec. 5 -6; Urban rent, site rent, Ch. XI; Ch. IX"]

Taussig: throughout question of value, you have phenomena varying amount equilibria. Marshall strong and basically equilibrium.

Suppose diminution of demand. Gradually through series of equilibria we have no adaptation.

Chart of Costs of Production of Raw Sugar.

See varying costs, some extraordinary high costs.

Elements in cost are two:

1. Producing raw material
2. Cost of conversation into raw sugar

Two schools average price and marginal prices. (Bulk-line Costs) or marginal price cutting out breaks. Others said cost price should be the price necessary for the majority of producers.

In manufacturing industries you have got some sort of curve. In former, Taussig put rice at margin, but in manufacturing cost it is more difficult.

1. Was not shown that low cost firms were same each year.
2. Information as to character of management and allocation of different items as cost. (Do you own or borrow capital) How had interest on capital entered?
3. Age of the firm – to aid in economic interpretation.
4. Did price over years approximate marginal manufacture or representative costs?

(England in Case of War
  See p. 412 – Quasi-Rent)

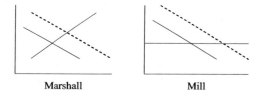

Marshall   Mill

Marshall and Taussig supply or demand alone do not determine price as Mill said. Mill assumed constant cost of production and then you do say that demand determine supply. Marshall says both blades of scissors cut. Marshall's thought is consistent. Quasi-rent emerges when demand suddenly shifts and exits under chain of equilibria of supply and demand. That part produced at cheaper prices yields Quasi-Rent for the time being. Does older distinction between rent on land and quasi-rent on instruments made by man. [In margin: "Bk. IV, Ch. 9, Sec. 7; Ch. 11, Sec. 1–2"]

Essential difference. (see p. 431) But practically land is not "permanently fixed." Urban land not limited, except in walled medieval cities.

See "Fetter" who says agricultural land not fixed, for purposes of economic fact.

But Marshall says, also, that supply of good land is fixed and not so with things made by land. There is limitation of best kinds of lands and the differential persists always.

Taussig says this point of Marshall inconsistent, because his previous analysis is presumes a differential in equality of the supply. Here he says supply is fixed, is akin to Mill.

War settlers in new country; the farmer banks on increasing value of land. This is postponed return for pioneer hardship and is not rent, says Marshall.

	I		II	
Building cost	100,000		New Building Cost	100,000 would yield
Land (rent				6,000
3,000	50,000		Loss on old	75,000 does yield
	150,000			4,500
Normal rental	9,000		Total outlay	175,000 total at 6%
Actual rental	4,500			9,000
Actual value	75,000			

III

New building cost   100,000

Rental   12,000

(Land rent 6,000)

Diminishing returns for urban land

German debate over duty grain. Anti-protectionists said that with application of scientific agriculture you had constant and not increasing return
over long time, but finally got increasing cost and decreasing returns.

Opposite said by Brentano. There is a stage of steep slope.

Rural Land

How about Urban Sites

First application of capital means low costs and high returns.

Ground floor is the money maker.

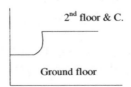

2nd floor & C.

Ground floor

Power and light have altered the situation in recent years. Hitherto had not paid to build high. Limit seems to be reached on sixth floor. But margin is reached.

Revert to figures. Under #(1),

1. Marshall would say 1,500 is quasi-rent as 3,000 you would get anyway. The quasi part depends on utility as it was constructed.
2. Old building torn down and new one put up. Shows it is cheaper to keep old building and the investment would pay the 1,500 for long time and would be normal. Explains why sites frequently are not used most advantageously.
3. Show how when population increases so that rental is 12,000 and rent is therefore 6,000 the new building would go up. There is here also quasi-rent, but in this case is above the normal.

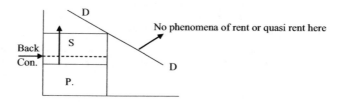

The quasi-rent is result of utility not cost.
Quasi-rent is what you get over and above what you have to get anyhow. But the prime and supplementary cost vary from firm to firm and so while some get quasi-rent others get true rent. Quasi-rent is result of price and not cause of it.

Quasi-rent conception – same sort of reason applicable to industrial plants. Value of a factory is the capitalization of the income and the excess over the outlay is the result not cause of value. Elements of business profits is large factor.

"Composite quasi-rent" (Shuman Corner) Quasi-rent for tenant as well as owner. Same holds true where you have an organization. (cf. Fuller Construction Co.) Where you have contention about the division of the quasi-rent, this concept of quasi-rent (Marshall's meteorites). Ease or difficulty of adjusting supplies determine which task is shifted or not. Steady tax over series of years different than tax for one year. Latter come out of quasi-rent.

Industry conducted under increasing costs

1. Distinction between internal and external economics.
   External economics – business aggregations.
2. Aneroid barometers – Will external and internal economics occur inevitable.
   Extension of demand will cause inevitably external economics (Brown and
   Sharp in Providence). These external economics are a cause of declining cost
   and declining price. Internal economics may result in increased demand in
   market sense through same economics effect all concerned.
3. Integration of industry.

Ch. XIII

Curve of diminishing costs – gives rise to differential element rent.

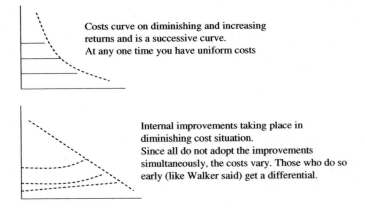

Costs curve on diminishing and increasing
returns and is a successive curve.
At any one time you have uniform costs

Internal improvements taking place in
diminishing cost situation.
Since all do not adopt the improvements
simultaneously, the costs vary. Those who do so
early (like Walker said) get a differential.

This explains the constantly vanishing business profit.

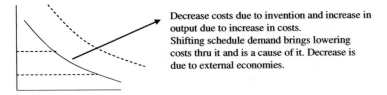

Decrease costs due to invention and increase in
output due to increase in costs.
Shifting schedule demand brings lowering
costs thru it and is a cause of it. Decrease is
due to external economies.

Internal economics uncertain but when they come they come rapidly.

External economics vice versa – they are predictable. As more cotton
mills develop, external economics develop. But this is a slow process.

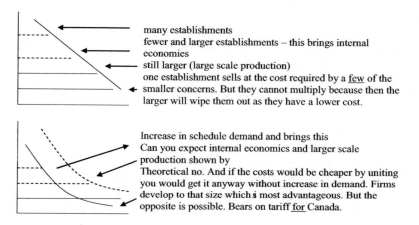

many establishments
fewer and larger establishments – this brings internal economies
still larger (large scale production)
one establishment sells at the cost required by a <u>few</u> of the smaller concerns. But they cannot multiply because then the larger will wipe them out as they have a lower cost.

Increase in schedule demand and brings this
Can you expect internal economics and larger scale production shown by
Theoretical no. And if the costs would be cheaper by uniting you would get it anyway without increase in demand. Firms develop to that size which s most advantageous. But the opposite is possible. Bears on tariff <u>for</u> Canada.

Doctrine of maximum satisfaction.

a. A tax does not bring in the amount lost in consumers surplus
b. A bounty does not bring in the amount it costs

Arise out of laissez-faire which has two entirely different connotations.

1. Refers to the material output (physical) [blank] people and more will be produced. Cornerstone of free trade (Adam Smith)
2. The thing of maximum satisfaction is different and says if people are free to consume what they want the production and price will be such as to yield maximum satisfaction.

> The older economists had this in mind too (Mill).

> In Marshall's diagram for increasing return it is possible by having S S^1 less steeply inclined to increase the net gain by a tax. Consumer surplus may be more if given to commodity produced under increasing return and the doctrine of maximum satisfaction would have been interfered with success. [In margin: "Read Care of Tax if Wars Came to England"]

> (Tax means only transfer – government hires people. Cause money to hire one service instead of another.)

Third possible connotation of maximum satisfaction:

3. It is most likely to be reached under equality of income. Equalitarianism flows from doctrine of diminishing utility.

<u>Maximum Satisfaction.</u>

[In margin: "F.W. Taussig & Pigou, Q.J.E., XXVII, 378, 535, 687" and "Pigou, Economics of Welfare, 263–267"]

This formal method has to be checked up by actualities of external and internal economics; incidence of taxation and economics importance of time. Marshall has in mind the "long run forces" particularly in bringing about external economics through shifting in demand curve.

Tax means tax upon individual and not the commodity.

Long time involved. Bounty must be put on long time so that it becomes a settled program, so that we can see the effect. Same thing with tax.

<u>Derived Demand</u> really means ultimate consumer – baking oven is derived from demand for bread.

<u>Joint Demand</u> – it is a form of derived demand (e.g., all the material going into the manufacture of a house)

Can you isolate these components of derived demand.

Application of this reasoning of Marshall on Plasterers. If one item is at constant cost the increase all goes to the other factor, e.g., if nod carriers can be in constant cost the bricklayers would get the whole increase arising out of shifting <u>demand</u> schedule to the right.

To get the <u>isolated supply price</u> you assume some information. You know the total or joint cost. The assumption is that you know the price of a substitute. (Packers vs. Federal Trade Commission.) Packers assumed that there joint supply price was a competitive once, whereas it was not so and this was one trouble.

<u>Application of Joint Costs and Joint Supply to theory of R. R. Rates</u>

Taussig had wanted it based on joint costs. But costs are not always joint costs in railroading. Back loading is an instance of joint costs. [In margin: "Marshall, Ch. 2 & 3, Bk. IV – Rent of Land."]

Difference between net and gross earnings of capital. Marshall divides it in three [in margin: "Bk. IV, Ch. 9, Rent of Land."]

a. Gross earnings
b. Earning of organization – required to bring entrepreneur and capital together

Capital   +   Marginal

Interest   Gross Profits   Profits

Marshall wanted to show profits are reward for ability and not reward for risk, as risk cannot be isolated. Another reason Marshall does away with risk is because it cannot be brought into equilibrium of supply and demand.

Nicety of adjustment of supply of managerial ability and its market price. Fundamental point in Marshall is that manager is he who with a given equipment go to the largest product and in his way the markets for management adjusts itself to a nicety. But he who makes the largest contribution in the long range view of things may not go to the top; as they may not command themselves to the market immediately because of inertia. And, when his point is accepted it has become a fact of common knowledge and a free good.

Fundamental difference between types of business open and closed to men of small capital:

    a. He must go into those business where he can make a quick turnover or haul.

    b. Must be a business where percent of fixed capital is small.

    c. Where new business methods can be introduced.

Why is it that in certain field of merchandizing the profit on turnover is higher than is more other business and what is the effect of the high profit on turnover upon competitive conditions, that is the number of stores.

Relation of Risk to Income from Management.

Walker's Captain of Industry has disappeared. He is the modern promoter. In law, corporation is like political democracy. But this is far from true as stockholders are rather beneficiaries and directors are like trustless. Germans say: law is form, economics is the substance. Much legal fiction in present legal corporate doctrine. Who is the entrepreneur in the corporation, cf. F.Y. Edgeworth's attempt in *Q.J.E.* some 20 years ago.

Capitalist always has alternative (opportunity costs). But does this count for much in life of individual worker. Stockholder can always hold out. Those quoted on Exchange always have opportunity costs. Choice respecting risks and degree of risks may be more real in case of capitalists than in case of labor.

Note difference between stockholders and bondholders. Owing something and being owed something.

Difference between profits on turnover and profit on investment effects of maintaining prices on competitive conditions; two kinds

   a. Small margin

   b. Large margin of profit.

In case of b small business can thrive. (cf. Dipley [unidentified] – Laws of Supply and Demand.) Are profits a capital category or entrepreneur category.

   We waive net earnings of management.

   How about gross earnings – do they belong to capital or to entrepreneur.

   (Capital and entrepreneur – can they be separated. English view is that they cannot; American view is that they can.)

Marshall says entrepreneur has a supply price. But has it a price in the sense that it can be increased. Marshall's analysis leads one to believe that he thinks it can be increased by attracting men of ability. Marshall assumed a freedom for that operation. But entrepreneurship may be beyond the control of supply pride. Entrepreneurship may be an inherited thing.

<u>Rent.</u>

<u>Define Diminishing Return:</u>

"decreasing physical product per increasing doses of capital and labor." See p. 150 Marshall. It runs in physical product terms. Is Marshall's definition sound?

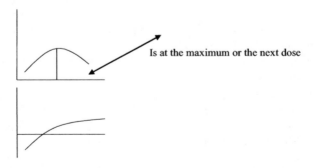

Is at the maximum or the next dose

Inherited properties of the land: heat, light, sunshine, space, rainfall, soil and qualities. Ricardo called them "original and indestructible powers of soil" and these are not so. [In margin: "Wages references to differences, Marshall – Bk. VI, Ch. 4 & 5."]

If you put "location" the diminishing returns on urban land comes in terms of "value" rather than in physical product, in which Carver rent and also diminishing returns.

Is the unearned increment unearned? There are two factors:

[In margin: "Cairnes on Leading Principles Non-Competing Groups, Part I, Ch. 3, Sec. 5 & 7."]

1. The growth of the value has been discounted in the rental accepted.
2. The future has been discounted in sales.

But reply is made that it is "unearned" because no economic energy has been put forward. Unearned increment is part of supply price of the ability of the homesteader.

> A single taxer urges that land are held idles to get the unearned increment and to bring them into use by taxing the vacant. (Is part of the unearned increment part of the supply price of the building.)

Unearned Increment.

Taxation of land values with exemption of improvements tends to force unused land into improvement. The tax decreases the land values for by forcing land on the market there may be still a further depression in price.

Income from land of two sorts:

a. Rental
b. Unearned increment

Take away b, you may remove inducement to hold land.

> "The Davenport paradox" proved it was impossible to tax land values. He has abandoned the position. Fallacy is that government would be getting rent instead of tax when it followed Davenport and taxed a parcel at 100%.[20]
> Young thinks building would be concentrated by the tax and some land forced out of rather than into use.

Can land be created? (cf., Boston 100 years ago) Was the Back Bay produced. (Marshall says it cannot) If rent is a return per physical unit (form) then we have a clue, even though we put rent in a % of the profit.

Fetter's (and Fisher's) argument that Pacific N.W. Railroad case made the land available and Fetter would say that is production, as only production which counts is production of values, just as mining is production. It is a case of creation of time utility.

Questions:

1. Different notion of Marshall and Ricardo on diminishing returns.
2. If you produce land by bringing it nearer the market may you not be said to produce land when you drain, plow or fertilize it.
   1. Ricardo was interested through Corn Laws in the high prices of rent. "Rent was high because wheat was high" said the economists. Ricardo on diminishing return had in mind agricultural diminishing returns. Join this with central doctrine of Malthusianism and you get economic pessimism. There was at that time many rent committees in Parliament. Ricardian theory of rent was explanation of fact and he was thinking of extensive (marginal land) farming rather than intensive. Quintessence of classical economy is found in Mill's chapters on the Stationery State.
   Marshall interested in the law of variable proportions which is universal in economics. Diminishing returns is playing an increasing part in economics; in some theories it is the backbone so far as distribution is concerned; and so it is no longer of historical interest alone. It operates all the time, here and now, and not alone in long times. Ricardo did not view it this way.
   2. The land owner determines how far cultivation goes by his demand for rent.

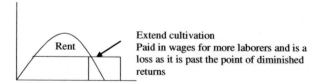

Rent

Extend cultivation
Paid in wages for more laborers and is a
loss as it is past the point of diminished
returns

This is same as point of view of minority in Sankey report[21], that wages should be paid out of what formerly was rent. In illustration, the marginal product is way below the wage paid. Deals with the question of the social utility of private property.

Returns to Labor

Marshall's point is equilibrium of supply and demand price. Does labor response to supply price.

Differences between labor and commodities – see Marshall 569.

1. Laborer owns himself. Implications for econ, theory, so far as efficiency of labor goes.

   a. Unless it is used today it is not used – it is perishable. But are they all lost. Note fatigue. Also where working life is short, it may not be true.
   b. The money invested in laborer depends upon his parents, their money and vision and foresight, says Marshall.
   c. Varying routing in various establishments, so far as advancement is concerned. This is an important economic problem.

See Footnote: analogy between earnings and rent is there marginal labor, or is income got by superior ability same as rent. [In margin: "Taussig 7 and 49"]

Cairnes on non-competing groups. Accepted in outline Ricardo and Mill and criticized them very thoroughly and rented their theories according to his views. But he is usually hairsplitting but is a keen critic.

What is he driving at in competing groups. Carnes objected to Mill's statement of cost of production being advance to labor and says it is based on labor, abstinence and risk. Cairnes says economists fell into trap because they took their concepts from capitalists and business man. Bagcheat [likely Walter Bagehot] said same thing. Cairnes influenced American economists at this point of cost of production, especially anti-Ricardians, particularly insofar as they criticize Ricardo, Mil and even Marshall because they say by cost they mean accounting cost and not social costs. Cairnes was first to note this.

Cairnes believed we had to get away from entrepreneurs costs (namely wages) and get something else. The difficulty is when measuring labor cost (skill, exertion) is that you have no way to measure sacrifice other than through wages, as you have no criterion of measurement. Some men are paid more for pleasanter and less arduous work. Cairnes' way not of difficulty was to way there was no free competition.

What are the non-competing groups according to Cairnes – (get it)

   a. Labor-unskilled
   b. Semi-skilled
   c. Professional men – ample means
   d. Special ability men

This classification is drawn in social terms rather than economic.

Capital is free to compete than labor.

<u>What does he do with the groups.</u>

1. Within the group sacrifice cost determines value. Cairnes was probably
    not thinking of subjective sacrifice cost. Is "cost: absolute or relative.
    That leads to opportunity costs; namely the cost is what you expend over
    and above what you would have expended at something else available.
    But do we know what the other expenditure in the alternative would have
    been. With opportunity costs, we could not get anywhere. To determine
    social costs, e.g., pleasure and rain economy.

    Young says in planning life there is one thing which is given –time in
    which we have to organize our life. So for each individual you get a kind
    of cost unit, such as say hour or week. What time is worth depends on the
    individual and the alternatives suggested. Can this be used to determine
    costs? It has a significance for social economies rather thin entrepreneur
    economics, says Young.

2. As between non-operating groups value is determined by reciprocal
    demand. This is Cairnes' statement of Mill's doctrines on international
    trade. Mill developed these doctrines on special value because labor is
    immobile, especially on international lines. Mill thought capital and
    labor locked up within national lines and international values could not
    be determined in ordinary way, where labor migrated to iron out dis-
    parity. [In margin: "Marshall, Bk. VI, 142; Marshall's general view of
    distribution"] Taussig's view on non-competing groups. (He builds upon,
    extend and revise Cairnes' theory.) Taussig has five instead of four. Basis
    of clarification is social criterion. Cairnes' criterion is intelligence, skill
    and training. It happened that lower groups (less honorific) get more
    money. Taussig suggests that a change may be occurring that attaches
    more honor to labor.

Principles upon which wages within these groups depend. Cairnes' has said the
principle was the fixed principle of Reciprocal demand. Taussig adds another. He
says demand for labor is derive demand and supply being fixed relatively for a
short time. Wages determined by increase in demand, and this is called "marginal
efficiency of the laborer." Cairnes is more fixed theory than Taussig's. Taussig
says depends upon (slight differences of ability in vast differences as, e.g., ε_1 time
R_1 as compared ε_2 time R_2.

If you count earnings of manager as function of ability and opportunity it is
easy to see that increase in demand for the product increases his earnings.

Difference between expenses and costs. Get it in Taussig

Is it desirable that difference between skilled wage and unskilled wage. Difference, Taussig says, should be small as that is socially desirable. Taussig says immigration has kept wages down.

Has immigration pushed up the common native – born labor?

Difficulty in the theory of distribution of the older writers; (see Marshall, Bk. VI, I, 1) How did Ricardo get around in his labor theory of value the difficulty when capital is present. He does so by assuming constant tax proportions of both so that did not harm his statement that things exchange in proportion to their labor cost. Ricardo also simplified it by taking of products at the margin to eliminate rent.

Difference between Ricardian and "Iron Law of Wages" of the Socialists. Is there any? In Ricardo's theory the Malthusian doctrine is an important promise. Lasalle said wages tend to a minimum of subsistence but is there a minimum other than conventional minimum?

Is it fair to say that marginal product of labor determines wages?

Marshall would accept this, but says that value of the marginal product depends upon the demand for that service. (But Webb says labor may not get its full product and collective bargaining enables him to get it.) In short-time view T.U. is able to throw over marginal productivity theory, and they raise the margin.

What do we mean we say marginal product determine wages.

$$\text{According to Clark} \qquad \text{MP} = \text{cause}$$
$$\text{Wage} = \text{effect}$$

[In margin: "Clark, Ch. I, II, III – Have you justified the social order when you provide that labor gets what it produces?" III, note specially difference between statics and dynamics. cf. Marshall's long time and short time. Omit IV, V, VI, and pass to VII, VIII, and IX."]

Marshall's view is that forces which determine wages are focused at the margin – a reciprocal determination. Marshall says marginal product relative to everything else.

On what does Marshall suggest that remuneration of any sort to laborer is superfluous. In cases of genuine fatigue.

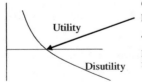

Continuance of work a matter of indifference. He is paid for keeping up and crossing the line.

Then he works until the last moment of work provides enough satisfaction to offset the moment of irksomeness

The curve may start below the line and show initial difficulty. But the laborer not guided by momentary state at the margin but being human he is guided by experience and is guided by the whole curve. He estimates the irksomeness upon experience.

Patten [unidentified] says man will stop before point of marginal utility arises because the thing which he buys he has not time to use.

This is fundamentally a matter of opportunity cost. The real cost is not fatigue and disutility itself is relative term and must be measured by alternatives. This is a relativist view of economics; there is nothing absolute. This assumes of course that choices are possible.

We pick and choose at the margin and back of that is opportunity cost.

Clark:

Ethical significance of specific productivity. Clark says: "men ought to get what they produce." Is this an adequate justification for the system? (Recall that ethics deals with individuals and the marginal product goes to function.) Does this follow, or if we justify rent do we justify the earnings of the individual landlord (note p. 8). Clark's ethical standard goes to his long-times (static) conditions.

The static state. The general line of progress looks like

The static state at any point such as A is the tangent to the line at that point. The static state is the culmination of forces now at work. Young says static state could exit if the whole relationship remained the same but only amount changed.

Marshall makes his system depend on supply and demand, and uses the margin to focus the problem. Clark is less eclectic than Marshall. Clark is simpler, more direct – it is marginal productivity.

Another difficulty with the ethical standpoint is that consumers are assessing values which determine what and how much shall be produced, in other words our values and schemes of life are institutional. Largest waste in economic sense is producing things which judge by any rational standard are not worth producing.

Difference between static and dynamic state.

> Have inventors any place in the static state? Static state has all adjustments made and there is no friction. There can be no changes in fashions, styles, demands.

> Where would Clark's static state fix in which Ricardo's Natural State, which dealt with long-time conditions? Static means long time period and not a short time period as something. Clark's wage theory is minimum subsistence wage and is long-time price.

Clark's Marginal Product of Labor.

> Where is it? It is labor using marginal capital by which Clark means no-rent capital or machine just worth using. Its relation with Henry George. George et al. had said the presence of free land had kept wages high. Does Clark accept this theory? (The settler expects the "unearned" increment.) If this is true can you say that vacant land determines marginal wages? Does Clark say the $[ax + bc] + \Delta x$ ran on the frontier that ax is equal to marginal wage or is the sum of $ax + bx$ the marginal wage; where the sum of the two is equal to x he earned before migrating. The bx is the expected "unearned increment; and the sum of $ax + bx$ give the marginal wage. But Clark by invoking the "unearned" increment may be calling in a dynamic feature in his static state. George left out the bx.

Specific product of labor is found

> It is distinguished.

> Is the marginal laborer any kind of laborer?

> Does marginal productivity mean value of amount of product?
> > (The organizer creates a value product.) His diminishing returns a physical or value returns. You cannot fix the law by appeal to physical quantities only.

> The laws formulated by classical economists were cost laws. A standard of life was element is cost of production of labor. This you don't find in Clark's static state because the population is given.

Capital and Capital goods.

Capital is capital in general and is an abstraction like the color green. It is not concrete. What's the difference between it and capital value? Clarks does speak of capital value but his "capital" is not capital value and differs from Fisher's and Fetter's Capital Value. But what is his "capital" if it is not the value of his capital goods. Capital value goes when the good goes but Clark's Capital does not so disappear. The capital of which then factory is the Capital goods, does not wear out.

As the profile (in the static state) being equal, there is an amortization fund. (Criticism of marginal production stuff that there is just as much cooperation at the margin between the various agents as elsewhere on the curve. Is the marginal product "an heroic abstraction?" Young says from the standpoint of the critic we cannot speak of economic activity. Pushing "the one-thing-at-a-time analysis" too far you get into trouble.) Labor also comes to be the abstraction which capital is. Labor is constant in the static state.

Clark's marginal product is "the value of a technical product" as you cannot find the marginal product by looking at physical facts along, as it is also determined by what the margin may sell for. Clark speaks of one of indifference to preclude mathematical discussion.

Clark is careful not to formulate law of diminishing utility in terms of quantity only, but as a joint result of quantity and quality. [In margin: "Ch. 21, 22, 24"]

Clarks' manipulation of Marginal Utility:

Earlier Clark has substituted capital – neither money value of goods, etc. – but something permanent, like the deathless corporation. A capital concept like this has significance only in the static state, and that state is the outcome of dynamic conditions and is the goal of those conditions. [In margin: "J.H. Wicksteed started with Jevons, Americans started with Austrians."]

(Read Chapter on Social Labor – which is to labor what Capital is to capital goods.) [In margin: "Economics of Enterprise; Davenport, McMillan"]

What is unique in Clark's concept of marginal utility?
    An apple is not value unit – it is a conglomeration of value units to Clark – such as color, appetite, durability, etc. The marginal money

you put in auto goes to these varying qualities. There is a fund of these utilities in the market. Standardized goods would not meet Clark's point – e.g., water, wheat, cotton. Supply and demand show well in sale of such produce on the open exchange. Clark begins at other end of series with multiplication of utilities, and differs in this respect from most economists. Clark speaks of color, legibility contents and Taussig and Marshall speak of books. Clark's scheme applies to non-divisible and non-standardized goods on the marginal utility device and Taussig and Marshall's analysis may not when you deal with the purchase of one unit. But Clark is not real – that's not the way things work.

Economic Causation.

1. Whether or no labor is robbed of anything. Line of Clark's argument goes as follows:

As the number of laborers increased from 50 to 100 the marginal (specific) product is lessened for each laborer for all produce alike and equally. Specific product (Young says) implies notion that you deal with laborers one at a time. The specific product is what the last laborer adds.

The specific product is not an additive thing – what one produces the other does. But Clark's social labor is the unit and Clark's present analysis deals with individuals.

2. Land & Capital. Why did Clark refuse to make of land a separate category; because he says there are only two things, rent and interest, which are two aspects of one thing. Capital and capital goods. Rent goes to capital goods. Fetter and Fisher also object to distinction between land and capital. Wicksteed also.

Fetter and Fisher have similar systems. In them rent is annual price for their use (usnace).

Capital Goods ⟶ $\dfrac{\text{Quantity}}{\text{Rent}} = \dfrac{\%}{\text{Interest}}$ ⟶ Capital Value

Capitalization depends upon rate of interest.

They are closely akin to Clark. They differ from Marshall greatly. According to Fetter Capital is capitalization of net earning. Marshall said capital determined by what it cost labor plus abstinence. For Fetter and Clark good will is also capitalized.

Clark is not concerned much with supply price because in a static state it is not important. Static state assumes a given amount of Capital, Labor and Land, and a given demand. Clark says what any piece of land gets is its specific product. Young says static is state of equilibrium, and is outcome of dynamic conditions.

3. Questions

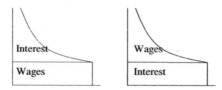

a. What is there to make us sure that wages = wage and interest equals interest in the two figures.
b. Can we talk of units of productibility; Land is like Capital for both can be reduced to units of productibility.

Clark identifies rent and interest as well as land and capital and is counter to classical view.

To Marshall rent was a differential.

Difference between capital goods and land. Clark allows for marginal capital goods – possibly capital of the marginal capitalists.

Can you put your finger on the marginal capital goods or marginal capital savers? Young says there is marginal capital – not so sure about capital goods. Pere Marquette example of marginal capital goods. You can find the marginal machine. To cf. land and capital you must find the gradation from the margin. In a static state every machine would be a marginal capital good as it would pay for itself and is just worth using. There are differential elements and yield a rent. Clark is thinking of short-time rent while Ricardian rent is long-time view. The rent in case of capital goods to conform to the rate of interest, and that rate determines what the rent shall be. In this case interest determines rent. In Clark's static his capital good are replaced.

Clark says land is transferred from group to group and these groups compete for land and this is opportunity costs. The English economists were thinking in the terms of grain and therefore no opportunity costs.

Ricardo said rent does not increase price while Clark says it does. Classical economist referred to supply and demand for short-time price. From this point of view rent enters into price in the short-time point of view.

Rent and product or supply are <u>alike</u> to Clark:

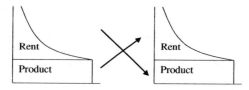

Are the margins like the extensive margins of the classicists?

Was this what classic talks about. <u>For them, rent was a long-time</u> thing or natural price and did not enter into cost, i.e., the short-time supply and demand price. Young says that American critics have set up a straw man.

<u>What is the Economic absolute or ultimate standard?</u> Clark measures it by disutility.

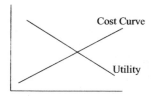

Why does Clark find it on the cost curve rather than on utility curve? Clark says cost of acquiring goods – sacrifice – is the unity. Goods are worth the labor it saves you from. For Clark it is the cost of acquiring the goods. The curves cross at the last working hour in the day. Does the 14th hour have to come at 6 or 8 pm. Not to be confused with ordinary psychological facts. The clock measure and physiological term must not be confused. Can you dissociate disutility of work and utility of product?

Can this standard be used in measuring value from year to year, or does it apply only to a static state?

Clark on Land.

It is not so much the acreage as its productive power. The English economics talk of land being fixed in area. Clark's view is the left wing view. Clark must determine whether to figure the power in value or unite, but here the difficulty is that physical production is a function of value. What is the physical production of the land? Secondly, how compare the physical products of lands differently situated, e.g., paying out coal to haul it. Danger is that the reasoning may be circular. Clark et al. say rent does enter into cost.

Young says capital and labor cannot be reduced to units of productive power, for the latter is an abstraction. What the market does is to buy and sell acres of land and not units of productive power. Reducing to units of productive power is begging the question says Young.

Reducing to units of production power leads as corollary that land can be produced – railroads, subway. But that is talking in terms of truisms. From a short-time view there are capital goods, just worth using. But in static state all capital good are like that. But here your capital goods is given data and the question is one of use.

Can labor be put in same crucible like land from Clark's point of view. Is there marginal labor and therefore rent of the super-marginal labor. Young says they can be found on forms. Can you divide the individual into differential utilities.

Clark, Wieser and Böhm-Bawerk said distribution all could be explained by law of rent generalized. German economists showed a differential element in wages and profits.

Ricardo said land rent could be determined from the intensive margin. They also suggested rent could be determined from the extensive margin. So far as extensive margin is concerned, Young says it holds and Young says there is marginal labor, which is just worth using. But that labor margin is different because there is the question of wages itself, which needs a subsistence level, but the extensive one is a cost-determined margin.

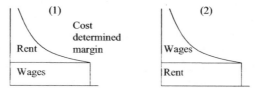

Young says #2 is essentially dynamic and unfair to use it in a static state.

Clark's Last Chapter [in margin: "Davenport, Ch. 2–3 is point of view. Restates Economics from standpoint of business. Akin to Wicksteed. Not so radical as Clark, Ch. 6 and 8."]

Clark's position on profit. None in a static state. In a dynamic state they tend to zero.

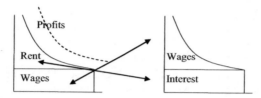

In the static state the price of finished product exactly equals labor and interest. There are no profits. In dynamic state there is divergence between profits and the whole product noted by dashed line. Arises out of good will, market opportunity, etc. or you sell product for more than goes to interest and wages. In a static state competition eliminates profits in one or other or both of two ways.

a. The invention may become common property – benefits diffused.
b. Selling the whole business (capitalization) for what it is worth.
   Profits disappear by becoming capitalized.

Schumpeter (Vienna) has gone Clark one better, postulating – interest is a derivative of profits and comes out of profits. Competition tends to destroy profits. With this tendency to disappear interest is a dynamic phenomenon and is non-existent in a static state. To prevent this, business constantly changing – Krupps, Remington Supply, Price of Capital – payment for abstinence – has nothing to do with it as there no demand price.

Could Walker be fitted into Clark on his no-profits man or his differential capitalist. Marshall included under profits, interest, payment for risk, wages of management, and a residual element. Clark would say you would have to charge into coat your own wages and that would come in wages. Clark is concerned with pure profits. Partial rapprochement possible.

Clark rejects risks theory of profit. Entrepreneur bears no risk that is borne by capitalists. Risk attached to capital and Clark would say also to small degree to labor. Entrepreneur as such does not risk. Profits to Clark are the results of enterprise. (They arise in a dynamic state by friction.)

Marshall's quasi-rent is a point of view. It is point of view. Quasi-rent disappears gradually as interest.

The benefits of progress accrue to the laborer. Here Clark as one with Walker in "Labor's residual Claim." Clark says wages get higher and interest lower and profit disappear. Young question the lowering interest. But Clark has loosened up only one factory. The thing would not happen if, say, population grew.

DAVENPORT

His system runs in terms of price – money plays dominant part. Opportunity cost is the corner stone.

Relation of costs to price. Costs affect value only as they affect supply. Mill and Ricardo said past costs did not affect the supply. Classicists said actual price fluctuate about the natural (long-time) price.

Affected through labor and capital leaving unprofitable lines. Costs work through supply. High pro its stimulated supply. Davenport deals with short-time price like most American economists. (Davenport emphasizes that classical supply and demand analysis subordinated question.) Davenport is in a perfect market rather than fictitious market.

With cost accounting are not costs becoming dominant?

Classicists thought of norm toward which prices tend. Davenport thinks of costs not as a norm but as a fact.

Under constant costs – cost of production does not affect price. Demand only then works.

Difference between maximizing pleasure and minimizing sacrifice (p. 59)

Former only adequate where both alternatives are pleasant – the second is universally true.

Doctrine of two margins: Davenport says production stopped when first of two margins is reached – that is an opportunity margin. He may quit fishing to rest or to hunt. Young says you can bring in to one margin – that is combine all other opportunities. How could there be more than one margin?

Is opportunity costs any more than economic relativism and puts you nowhere? Davenport in back of his head absolute pain costs. Take all different uses of time and make leisure a collective thing, then you can use that leisure as alternative and so the opportunity cost.

Is there a difference between opportunity costs and other costs; note the case of stock sold at 110 and then going to 150. Does this differ between that and loss incurred if sold at 90. Do you need to distinguish between positive and negative loss?

Classicist economist spoke of costs and looked backward. Davenport looks forward.

Opportunity costs of Davenport found in Ricardo and his followers in the shape of the doctrine of comparative costs. Trade between different countries would be determined by the comparative costs and not by absolute costs. Opportunity cost is a special application of that doctrine. This is the doctrine of international exchange. This assumed immobility of labor and capital. This can now be questioned as to capital; not as to labor. Other school of critics of comparative costs says it holds in national as well as international. Young says in international trade long time and short time important for the movement of labor and capital as the flow is more sluggish. Classical economists spoke of a generation as a long time. From standpoint of international trade that might be a short time. So Davenport's viewpoint is a short-time view. (Marshall tired to consider both long-time and short-time view.)

What are profits to Davenport?

The Cost Schedule.

How about the interest charge which is included. Davenport's purpose is to show how a man reasons to find out whether he should go into business (can you apply opportunity costs to profits) which is a cost accounting purpose. (From standpoint of entrepreneur rents do enter into costs but not from standpoint of society.) Minimum profit to Davenport are those that are equal to opportunity costs. (See Davenport, p. 68.)

Thoroughgoing application of opportunity costs to cost must show how to compare 10% chance and 200% gain and 75% chance and 20% gain. Depends upon individual psychology. After all profits are what you have still to get. To go as far as Davenport seems to deny the "risk view" of profits. He really counts two unknowns. [In margin: "Ch. 6, 7, 8, 9, 11, 12, 13, 18, 19, 28."]

Davenport on Demand

How does he differ on this? His analysis of marginal utility depends on two causes:
   a. Various desires which compete. One can compete only at the expense of others.
   b. The law of satiety.

The latter has received attention from economists. The place is found in the market where you buy for today and tomorrow. Davenport introduces "relative marginal utility" termed subjective worth or value of other economists. Young says this is Marshall's marginal utility. Relative marginal utility is question of choices. Is the utility curve any more than a displacement curve, and is marginal utility itself any more than a way of expressing opportunity cost.

Who sinks the raft – the last man or the group? Is there any relation with this and productivity. It is just as hard to distinguish the marginal unit. You cannot do it. In a sense the 10 men sink it, but this is no more than saying that the raft sinks with 10 men. The 10th man is any one of the 10, and he causes it to sink.

Is the marginal pair of bargainers more significant than any other pair? Now we pass to buyers and sellers. Our units are not homogenous. We talk not of unite but of marginal buyers and sellers. Are the buyers on the margin more important that the others? Yes, they are, as they affect supply and through it, price.

[Crossed-out graph of an upward sloping supply line and a downward sloping demand line here.]

But for flour there is no marginal buyer, but there is a marginal unit.

What is Capital to Davenport?

It is durable property or wealth expressed under the price denominator. Would Davenport include consumption goods as do Fisher and Fetter. These latter figure these goods as service income over time. Davenport would also include consumers goods, but possibly not on Fetter's ground of psychic income.

Fisher & Fetter pass by to easy transition from individual capitalization to the total. (Davenport rules out personal capacities? Davenport's is a system of the industrial system.)

Fisher and Fetter go direct to market rents and rates while Davenport holds individual assessment. Affects market rates only through the individual's reservation price.

Davenport includes land in capital. So it enters into pride, because his costs are entrepreneur's costs. But if they are not entrepreneur's costs what are they? Also from opportunity cost viewpoint, land costs and enters into price. (Quasi-rent is recognition of difference between long-time and short-time view.) You cannot sum opportunity costs no more than weight solar system. For society as a whole opportunity costs cancel one another. So for a national economy you cannot use them. (Ricardo said rent is deduction from annual income of a country.) (Malthus said rent is increase from annual income of a country). From a national, as opposed to entrepreneur point of view, rent is neither and involves only transfer – it is a distribution of income. Can you say the same about the other factors? Apply this to alternatives – or opportunity cost. Are there not national choices?

(Pigou's chain Wealth – Welfare – States of Consciousness – and then into ethical concepts.)

On what ground does Davenport kill supply and demand curves? Davenports says they both amount to some thing; two views of same thing. Note the reservation price. Wicksteed has same doctrine – market consists of buyers. Marshall's market consists of commodity and money.

To find an economic absolute you got to get away from money economy. You can find it only in pain or pleasure. But no efforts successful.

[In margin: "Knight, Part II, 3, 4, 5, 6"]

Wicksteed "Common Sense of Political Economy" does not emphasize so much difference between competitive and social point of view. General view of supply and demand and costs akin to Davenport. Wicksteed insists that self-interest or the opposite lies at bottom of economics. He says there are not economic categories but ethical categories – evaluation. "My relations to other are impersonal – I buy at the lowest and sell at the highest. I am not concerned with persons. Ethical question arises only when you ask "What are you going to do with money?" In other words, purposes alone involve that decision. But methods of acquisition have no ethical content. Wicksteed derives from Jevons.

Davenport on Abstinence.

Senor had developed the doctrine to round out the labor theory of value.

What is the trouble with the abstinence doctrine. Davenport says it involves the hedonistic calculus.

One-sided view of interest; abstinence and (2) productivity, and to some extent Davenport is one-sided on productivity – also Fisher, Wicksteed.

Is abstinence a cost which must be paid? Classical view was that society works through factors: land, labor and capital. Capital from labor + abstinence. So factors are land, labor and labor + abstinence. Davenport says there is capital in business which did not cost abstinence. He includes land and waterfalls, but that not fair to classicists. Davenport realizes that many goods are produced not in a way in which land is produced – without abstinence. From short-time point of view they are there whether we pay interest or not.

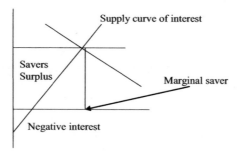

Marshall says interest that must be high enough to induce the marginal saver. Davenport says not even marginal saver is entitled to interest.

Although Knight aligns himself with Mill and Marshall in many respects more radical than American "dimensions," any new idea can be found in Marshall. Modern economics is a primary economics.

Knight's Utility – it is a matter of choice – opportunity costs. Sometimes Diminishing Utility represented as diminishing sensation as the stimulus increases. Geometric stimulus and arithmetic sensation. Other points of view – put consume in the market and not at the dinner table. Then he says – the more I have of this, the less I have of that. Utility diminishes because if I increase apples, I do without more bananas. Both illustrations used. Knight throws the "dinner table" out. Increasing pressure from other demands causes Diminishing Utility of apples depend upon demands of other things. Knight says for purpose of economics, pleasure and pain are relative.

Davenport discusses the same thing under "relative marginal utility." For Knight, it is not a question of psychology, but upon the point of view of the individuals.

[Seeing utility up with price has been evaded.]

Reservation prices for Knight are demand prices – same as Davenport.

Knight says D.R. [diminishing returns] for one factor means I.R. [increasing returns] for other factors. Knight's hypothetical society like Clark's Static State. Diminishing Returns – how does Knight diverge from others. When one factor gets diminishing returns same as saying, others get increasing returns.

   This is original with Knight and an important thing.

Factors of production. Classicists said law, labor and capital. Clark said labor and capital. Knight said labor not homogenous and uses law, labor and capital. Used only as tools, recognizing they are not homogenous – and we deal with concrete units. Knight would say there are thousands of factors of production.

Why does Knight put diminishing returns at point where is tangent to the line passing through the origin. This explains figure p. 100.

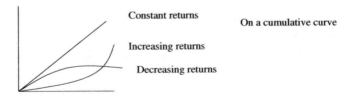

Constant returns

On a cumulative curve

Increasing returns

Decreasing returns

Where curve changes to D.R. from above is tangential to the straight line of constant returns because passing from increasing returns to decreasing returns momentarily at least you have constant returns.

Diminishing Returns is point at which returns to (say) labor increase less rapidly than that at which (say) laborers increases.

The proportional def. of diminishing returns

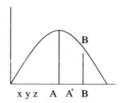

A' adds less than A but because x, y, z add so little that the real point is at B.

Hobson's Criticism. (Adrion and Davenport say the marginal product is just as much a product of all as any other product.)

Hobson's objection (see p. 113). Young says not much in Hobson's point, because man has a certain margin for experimentation but in large part slavishly imitates.

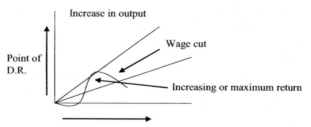

Where curve parallels wage curve, you have the margin. To get there, you <u>must</u> have concavity. This is important. Young recommends this type found in Knight.

D.R. is point at which an added increment of factor makes a less than proportionate increase in product. This is Mq view.

Where increment of factor adds less to product than previous unit. This Ma view

[illegible graph here]

Knight is interested in proportionate way of going at this problem.

Empirical and a priori chance.

Lecture out

Next Monday last two chapters.

Why did classical school not adopt opportunity costs?

"Short-hand in concept of general rate of wages" also profits, says Young. Is there a "pure rate of interest?" How about insurance annuity or high grade government bond? Can you divorce interest from other things involved – such as expenses of supervision. Wages and purchasing power are changing. Can all contingencies be removed? Can risk or uncertainty be isolated? So does not interest (without profits) bring in static conditions. Pure interest a device for exposition. Profits and interest are inextricable and separation means logical abstraction.

Shape of risk curve

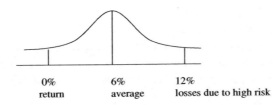

0%	6%	12%
return	average	losses due to high risk

Must the shape be normal or skew.

A long-time point of view of one concern would give different shape. Suppose the empirical curve is skewed to right – is it? No one knows.

Curve of Indifference.

Ordinates represent: probability. What curve do you need to render a man indifferent?

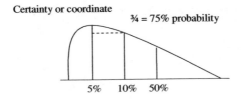

Can't say that particular man prefers 50% income and 100% chance than 10% return on 50–50 chance. Men do give in upper reaches more than the actuarial value of a range of problems not yet explored.

What and who is entrepreneur and his functions

a. Organizer
b. Risk taker
c. Administrator
d. Capitalist

According to different economists

Knight says – a risk taker. Carver has a risk theory. Knight classifies them. With insurable risks the entrepreneur does not deal. He deals only with uncertainty.

Young says entrepreneur buys agents of production and commutes them into things he sells on open market. Suppose he sells on contract and buys on open market.

There are technological risks.

There are opportunity risks (or negative risks)

(Differentiate profits on the turnover and "profits in the business). The function – entrepreneur – cannot attach to any one person.

Knight says entrepreneur is man who "plunge[s] into uncertainties". He either succeeds or does not.

"Responsibility and control" are also used; but responsibility attaches to the risk taker – but I am responsible to capitalists and the latter takes the risk. That is Clark's point of view, i.e., capitalists and creditors. Therefore responsibility is a better term in some ways.

Control means directing the various business opportunities. Idle to tie entrepreneur to single function or responsibility. Easier to classify types of income than functions of entrepreneur. (No profits in Knight's static state – he draws line between insurable and uninsurable risks. So far as change can be untold you eliminate profits. Clark thinks society stagnant so that be no profits– Knight says society must be know and predictable so that there be no profits. Clark's static state is the no-profits stage. (Profits – just happen)

Marshall emphasizes analogy between wages and supply prices of entrepreneur.

THOMAS NIXON CARVER'S COURSE IN THE DISTRIBUTION OF INCOME

ECONOMIC THEORY
PROFESSOR T. N. CARVER
FIRST SEMESTER
1921–1922

MAURICE B. HEXTER

ECONOMICS 12: CARVER

Oct. 3

Do market values coincide with social values?

People who have high purchasing power may give a high market value to articles of low or negative social value.

Are wealth and well-being synonymous?

If desires are vicious, well-being will not be thus synonymous.

Purchasing power must be earned. If they are not, market values will not coincide with social values; the system is at fault.

1. Income are unequal.
2. Desire are sometimes vicious; two factors which must be kept separate.

"Imaginary distinction between normative and positive"

"No distinction is of value unless it can be used"

Necessary is assume that desires are equal.

See 370–371, Henry Clay, Econ. For Central Reading

Oct. 5

Close connection between wealth in sense of goods and sense of well-being; relative; because well-being depends on goods. More of it equal more well-being equals wealth. Not a question of absolute. If there is anything we think we need, we try to get it – call it wealth.

Popular sense of word wealth (?) censorious idea of wealth, i.e., That people do not know what they need and therefore have a false notion of wealth. This censorious attitude is not democratic. It would imply that the market value of wealth is not the same as the social value.

Parallel case of economics and politics no reason for denying this.

Social utility does not increase in an amount necessarily proportionate to the increase of the good.

Granted the market valuation of social value is faulty, is there any other kind of valuation? Any other method? Is there any way of correcting this alleged fault without introducing worse evils? And this is a sort of doctrine of comparative costs.

Ex. Alcohol; Cost of repression. Is this cost out of proportion to the good achieved? Repressors as often mistaken as not. Irritation. Same applies to jazz music, bad business, etc.

Institutions are determined by the faces of the distribution of wealth, not vice versa.

Oct. 7

Market price as a test of social value. Is there a better test? If desires are vicious, market value will reflect this. Is there an alternative? Is political expression any more rational? Would a government, representing such people, be any more rational in setting values? – there is no more perfect means than market value, for determining social value, provided the desires of the people are fairly sane.

The difference in purchasing power does not affect this conclusion.

Social value needs to be considered, not in terms of the present alone, but of the future also – with regard to the needs of the great majority yet unborn. Social values should go to those who will transmit them, not to those who merely consume.

"It is highly immoral to borrow or lend for purpose of consumption." Interest is paid only in cases where the money lent adds to the volume of social value, by being invested wisely, either in person or through a bank. The money is lent to a man with a machine, thus both lender and borrower are benefited.

Oct. 7

Economic good are such as need to be economized. Involve choice.

Oct. 10

Question of unemployment brought up. Harvard Bureau of Ec. Res. shows that Government Bureau of Labor figure of 5 million unemployed is approximately one million too high, owing to inclusion of those employed in industry during war, now absorbed in domestic service, the farm and the home.

Absolute vs. relative employment.

Factor of reluctance to take less agreeable work than was formerly had, a minor but real one.

Industry will reopen only costs can be paid out or receipts. Lack of high business ability may be a contributory factor here.

Maneuvering for position of advantage in required reduction of prices has brought about a deadlock, which is the cause of the present unemployment, fundamentally. Furnishers of raw material want to see if freight rates will not be reduced; railroad men threaten to strike, that reduction in costs may not be from their wages.

"Unemployment" of Cape Cod cranberries during the sugar shortage an excellent analogy to the present unemployment situation.

Government control, or government employment. Based on taxation, thus lessening money in circulation to pay labor in private employ, and expenses of private industry. Government may start the return, by acting at psychological moment. But this may retard, instead of accelerating return to normal. If taxation in time of prosperity has given a surplus, then affects may not be had.

Human wants; "desire" most general term. Tropistic reactions. Psychological factors other than calculated self-interest very uncertain and hard to determine, such as patriotism, enthusiasm, etc.

Calculated self-interest has permanence that these other motives, instincts, etc., have not. It is a self-renewing desire. Social enthusiasm is not. Even a religious enterprise will not be successful unless appeal is made to calculated self-interest, thought it be to salvation in the other world.

Cooperative enterprises. What motive is involved? Only is Calculated self-interest – economic desire – is the motive, will the cooperative enterprise be successful. The manger is motivated by his salary prospects, the farmers by their gain.

No objection to basing this calculated self-interest on the instincts, but there is to the elimination of it as a fundamental.

Man is what he tends to become, rather than what he is. He tends to become rational. Why not call this the distinctive human quality, rather than the animal traits, as do the psychologists.

Oct. 14

The economist deals with desires, not as to their sources, but as facts of economic importance. These desires are self-renewing. Others do not give calculability to human conduct; with this predictability economics is primarily concerned – not as regards quantity so much as quality.

(Wants) Desire is satiable. Basic of marginal utility of things. Very important principle.

Desire is self-centered.

Economic principles and laws are not absolute, but is an equilibrium of forces. Nothing rests on anything definitely; everything is determined by a balance of forces.

So, though desire is self-centered, no human being is entirely self-centered in his desires. Every human thinks more of himself than of other people. He thinks more of people near him than he does of people far away, in time, space, kinship, likeness of mind. This nearness is self-centeredness. This kind of desire causes action work.

How does this self-centered desire work?, i.e., is it justified? Carver thinks, very well. It leads to balanced action, for man's energies can reach only those near him. Economic science demands that human interests necessary for well-being be looked after by those who can do it best. Who can do it best? By those who know the interests concerned best. Normally, those are best qualified who are nearest to the interest. This general interest are best looked after when each man looks after his own.

Oct. 17

Voluntary agreement among free citizens the means of settlement of disagreement. Any other weapon is wrong; especially so when these using such other weapons have reached a state of property equal to the average prosperity of the citizens of the country. It is wrong because it is a use of force to secure what would not be granted under any other conditions.

Oct. 19

Unions as a deterrent to enterprise.

Oct. 26

Lets not expect better bread than can be made from wheat, or government than can be made of men.

Tawney's "Acquisitive Society" – a very shallow book.[22]

Necessity of balancing political power against market power. Same motives in vote getting as in money getting.

Nov. 2

The incompatibility of a strike with governments.

Labor unions arrogate to themselves the function of government.

Carver believes that there never was a strike without violence, in order to keep others from taking their places.

Is a strike revolution?

If a thing is undertaken, knowing that certain other things will have to be done in order to accomplish the end, then these incidental things are essentially a part of the definition of the first. Thus with violence and strikes.

Nov. 7

Need for a more literal usage of terms. Instance; Marx' use of term "metamorphosis of capital", referring to "depriving" of workers of tools by capital. Word deprive misleading here; the process was one of advantage to the laborer, he could with the primitive tools he himself could command.

Capitals: Everything, all goods, save land, from which gets material income. Fisher would include most consumers goods, because they render an immaterial income. Household furniture, for instance. Most economists confine term to those goods yielding material income.

Money wage and real wages usually distinguished.

The mistake; Taussig and Hobson is in assuming that when we acquire something, no one else gets any good out of it.

Nov. 9

Nature and function of capital.

Böhm-Bawerk's observation on the superiority of roundabout process in production. Is this observation borne out? Direct process best under certain conditions, when small capital (instrument) is used, as in gardening. But even here, where capitalistic production is largely disposed there is much roundabout process, much preparation necessary.

Böhm-Bawerk says a rule, by empirical observation, the indirect process is best. Carver thinks better not say "a rule" – but that there are a large number of cases, by empirical observation.

The roundabout process requires waiting, on the part of someone, under any form of organization. There must be preparation for a crop, perhaps, of 10 years hence, or 1 year. The preparer may wait for his product, or society may pay him, and itself wait for the income.

Roundabout process sometimes advantageous; when it is, it requires waiting. This waiting usually means either preparation of movable capital, like ploughs, etc., or preparation of the soil, etc., by which its marketable value is enhanced or the possibility of crops increased.

Two questions:

1. Is waiting necessary?
2. Who shall do it?

All three of these methods of waiting are found in any community. If one more right than the other?

1. Should the laborer hang on to what he makes?
    i.e., Do his own waiting?
2. Shall the laborer buy his tools from someone else?
    i.e., Sell out and let someone else wait?
3. Should the State tax the people in order to make the tools, having the tax payer do the waiting?

Accept interest as a fact – why is it high rather than low. Then there must be reference to the psychological dislike of waiting. Productivity explains interest itself – the explanation cannot be made on a basis of psychology.

Nov. 14

The productivity of capital. Question as to that must arise only when a certain point of view, of capital as a fund of value (Clark, Fetter) is held. When capital is that of as tools, its productivity is obvious. Confusion between these two views leads to disagreement. Marx evidently held the former.

The growth of joint stock companies led to a confirming this erroneous former impression, because people thought of themselves as owning property which reflected value, rather than as owning the tools in question. The essential thing is thus observed.

Industrial Organization:

> "Mechanical" force in the inorganic world, "stimulator" in the organic, "appeal" in the super organic world of society.

> Need for some sort of an "appeal" to secure action in industrial affairs. The present system uses the appeal to some aspect of personal interest. Can other appeal be effective? Supposing we abolish "wage slavery" would there be any other resources than to authority, i.e., conscription to make man work.

> This is illustrated in Russia.

Nov. 16

As a spring to industrial action, shall the appeal be to hope of reward, involving a bargaining, or to fear of evil, involving command, force, threat. The first seems to be higher. Yet we should compare them on the basis of their extent, their whole curve of application, rather than on the basis of certain parts – say the best with the worst.

The process of development is from the fear of consequences (or from threat) to hope of reward. In nearly all orders, however, it will be necessary to fall back on the first at times. And after we have reached the second stage there are higher and lower categories of good to be offered as an appeal.

Eve in the highest scale, this principle of reciprocation, which is a king of bargaining, operates. Even divine love expects love in return.

Nov. 21

VIII

Equilibrium of demand and supply.

Clark; "Static State" complete fluidity without motion; no difference from Marshall's equilibrium.

Analogy between "balance of nature" and economic equilibrium.

This concept is Marshall's most important contribution. Depends on diminishing supply and increasing cost. Tendency toward this equilibrium always present. More difficult to see, than in biology, but present nevertheless.

Approach to economic problems must be on this equilibrium basis. An equilibrium price cannot be tampered with without introducing new and greater problems. No price fixing, therefore. Factors on one side or other if the equilibrium may be changed, and a new equilibrium – price thus formed. New methods of farming may be taught, for instance, or men may be induced to grow new crops. This is the most important principle of the last 100 years.

This readjustment always takes time, even where fluidity is very marked.

Minimum wage law; requires handling the surplus of labor in some way. If this is done, the law accords with the principle of equilibrium.

Furnishes basis of sound reform. Important. Any change in price – of capital, labor, goods, must take this into consideration.

Nov. 28

Problems; what is good? Institutionalism versus something else as the means of means of discovering. "Something" refers to objective tests.

Survival as a test of goodness, not absolute. What has survived has some good in it, and Carver places emphasis upon survival values.

Moral as survival value.

Nov. 30

1. Joint Demand

Note correspondence between this term and term complementary goods, for which there is always a joint demand.

2. Composite demands; opportunity cost – a certain correspondence of meaning.

Ex. In determining cost of milk, cost of corn, which might be used for grain rather than for fodder, must be considered. Thus there is a composite demand for corn.

Terms used by different economists often the same, or concerned with the same matter, only viewed from a different angle.

"Joint supply" equals by-products.

"Composite supply" equals substitutes.

Connection between Gresham's law and Marshall's conception of composite supply.

(Cheap money will drive out dear money – Gresham's Law)

Would cheap money drive out dear money if there were no legal tender? Carver says no – because if there no tender, gold, which has real value will be demanded and paper will not be accepted. Therefore Gresham's law depends on the presence of legal tender. It is really only a phase of the concept of substitutions.

Connection between wage-fund doctrine and joint demand.

Dec. 2

If everybody demanded gold, prices would tend to fall. Policy of Treasury Department during was mistaken.

Necessity of distinguishing between physical convenience and purchasing power in money. The amount of gold is reduced – then there is still plenty of purchasing power – but it would be physically inconvenient to handle it, so much value would be attached to a microscopic unit.

Every time you withdraw a federal reserve note, the value of gold increases, the price of commodities decreases. There is the same effect if people demanded gold at the banks (as Carver avers.).

Injustices to debtor or creditor the chief objection (Carver's) to the instability of prices. This is an important factor in bringing about crises.

Fisher's scheme for stabilizing the dollar. Carver rather approves testing – selective, value of cycles and business depressions. Renewed confidence in firms that survive.

Dec. 5

Increasing importance of substitution.

Direct and indirect substitutes; indirect satisfy alternative needs and the competition between then is nearly as been an between direct substitutes, which supply identical needs. An automobile or a trip to Europe – indirect substitutes, with a certain amount of competition.

Social implications of this; competition may exist between auto builders and house builders. (x) There are few, if any, necessary commodities at present. Brand is easily substituted for. Coal is perhaps the most necessary, but ever here, there are several different kinds.

Our attitude toward monopoly conditioned by a recognition of possibility of substitution. If monopoly were of real necessity, it would not be tolerated. As it is, we are indifferent.

Substitutes have an effect on elasticity of demand, in that they enable the consumer to shift from one thing to another. Demand is inelastic where there are few substitutes. Hence – does the consumer pay the tax or tariff? It may well be the producer, for the consumer can shift the something else. From the consumer's side, elasticity is largely a matter of substitutes, from the producer's it is largely a matter of substitutes, from the producer's, it is largely a matter of alternative markets.

The Retardation of Production:

> Due to either (1) Cost, that is Disinclination, as it is, always, in the last analysis, psychological, or (2) Monopoly.
>
> No other factors
>
> If there were no disinclination to save, interest would be unnecessary; if there were no disinclination to work, work would be costless. There is a good deal of saving that is costless – that is, it is done naturally and gladly, without thought of reward. Hence the return is a surplus, sort of rent. This is determined, however, by the usual
>
> Kinds of disinclination: (1) Fatigue cost
>   (2) Opportunity cost
>
> (2) is becoming more and more important.
>
> Disinclination to work, to wait, to save, beyond a certain point.

Dec. 7

Relation between monopoly price and substitutes; no such price if there are <u>direct</u> substitutes.

Monopoly has a very limited power at present owing to the multiplicity of commodities, allowing for substitution.

In case of formation of a great monopoly, Carver would rely, first, on a governmental requirement of a uniform price for a commodity, and second, if necessary, the fixing of a price, not necessarily based on cost of production, but rather in the nature of an equilibrium price. He would not try to regulate the actual formation of a monopoly, or prohibit it, by means of an anti-trust law.

A tax on commodities of a monopoly character would be passed on. Carver believes, to the consumer. A tax, graduated, on strictly monopoly profits could not so be passed on.

Generally accepted that a land-rent tax cannot be shifted. This is a pure surplus. Not hard to distinguish between the value of the land and that of improvements, but it is much harder to distinguish between rent for special ability and excess profits.

Dec. 9

Carver-Ec. 12.

If disinclination to wait were non-existent capital would accumulate to the point at which interest would disappear.

Dec. 12

Four fundamental propositions concerning capital; Mill.

Fourth most difficult, i.e., the demand for commodities is not a demand for labor. Connected with the wage-fund doctrine, then defended by Will.

Given a demand for commodities and a body of labor, a connection, such as that of entrepreneurs, who are willing to pay money to produce commodities, i.e., who have a wage fund — has to be consumed. Opponents of Mill assume this unconsciously. Mill insists upon making the assumptions consciously.

The wage fund depends upon the discounted productivity of labor; the wages depend upon the wage fund. Divide the wage fund by the number of laborers, and you get the average paid.

<u>Willingness of people to invest</u> is the link stressed by Mill as necessary if a given demand for commodities is to result in labor being employed. The mere demand itself is not enough.

The wage-fund doctrine comes under Marshall's concepts of joint demand and composite supply.

Differences in wages; why are some laborers paid more than others?

1. Cost element.
2. Cost of acquiring training or education in irksomeness or in positive spending and lack of earning.

Dec. 16

Artificial control of supply; apprentices; closed-shop
Ways of increasing wages

1. Decreasing supply of labor
2. Increasing demand for product

Dec. 19

Walker's position as to the question whether wages are paid out of past, present or future labor, was that they are paid out of future labor. In the sense that the employer is willing to pay because of the prospect of future production, this is true. But in a literal sense it is not true.

Anticipate future product, discounted, causes the employers to be willing to pay wages.

No employer can run a business without having a fund out of which to pay the laborers in advance of the appearance of the product on which they are laboring.

Dec. 21

Assuming a demand for an articles that is to be produced, and effective methods and machinery in production, the success of the business, individual or national, will depend on the proper balancing of the three factors of land, labor and capital – that is, in their proper proportions.

	Productivity Theory
Interest:	Abstinence Theory
	Equilibrium Theory; a combination of other 2.

A man borrows and is willing to pay interest, because he hopes to gain more than enough by means of the tools he buys, to pay the interest back.

The question as to whether capital is productive is identical with the question whether tools are useful.

Fisher's is a phase of the abstinence theory.

Interest induce saving – that is investment in productive enterprises. Without it, there would be much saving, but it would not be invested productively – it would take the form of hoarding, jewelry, etc.

NOTES

1 Silus Marcus MacVane of Harvard University was a frequent contributor to Taussig's *Quarterly Journal of Economics*. MacVane was born on Prince Edward Island in 1842. He received an A.B. degree from Acadia College, Nova Scotia, in 1865. MacVane served as an instructor in political economy, and later as an assistant professor and professor of history at Harvard before retiring in 1911.

2 T.E. Cliffe Leslie (1825–1882), leading figure of the English historical school, authored *Land Systems and the Industrial Economy of Ireland, England and Continental Europe* (1860), which was highly praised by J.S. Mill. *Essays in Political Economy* was published posthumously in 1888.

3 Ferdinand Lassalle (1925–1864) was a German-Jewish jurist and socialist political activist. Some credit Lassalle with having invented the phrase "Iron Law of Wages."

4 Rochdale Society of Equitable Pioneers was founded in 1844 as an early consumer co-operative in England. They are perhaps most famous for designing the Rochdale principles, or principles of co-operation that still provide the foundation for operation of some co-ops today.

5 David L. Friday (1876–1945), an instructor and professor of economics at his alma mater, the University of Michigan (1908–1921). In 1922, he assumed the presidency of Michigan Agricultural College in East Lansing. He left M.A.C. for the New School for Social Change in New York in 1923. Friday published on agricultural problems and problems of value in the *American Economic Review*, the *Quarterly Journal of Economics*, and the *Journal of Political Economy*.

6 James E. Allison, Commissioner and Chief Engineer, Public Service Commission, St. Louis. Ethical and economic elements in public service valuation. *American Economic Review*, 27 (1), 1912.

7 Perhaps Eugene B. Patton of the University of Chicago. Patton received his A.B. degree from Washington University in St. Louis and his A.M. and PhD from the University of Chicago. He taught at the University of Chicago and later Rochester University before becoming the chief statistician in the Department of Labor in the State of New York.

8 Refers to German chemist Baron Justus von Liebig (1803–1873), a pioneer or organic chemistry, including studies of soil fertility.

9 Petr Alekseyevich Kropotkin (1842–1921) was a geographer, a zoologist, and one of Russia's foremost political activists and anarchists.

10 Carl Ballod (1864–1931), German professor economics specialist in central planning. See Nicholas Balabkins. (1978). Der Zunkunftsstaat: Carl Ballod's Vision of a Leisure-Oriented Socialism. *History of Political Economy, 10* (2), 213–232.

11 Edmund E. Day, "An Index of the Physical Volume of Production: I. Agriculture, 1879–1920," "An Index of the Physical Volume of Production: II. Mining, 1879–1919," "An Index of the Physical Volume of Production: III. Manufacturing, 1889–1912." *Review of Economics and Statistics, 2* (9, 10, and 12) (1920). Day (1883–1951) was an economist at Dartmouth, Harvard, Michigan, and Cornell, where he also served as president (1937–1949). He published extensively on statistical measures of production.

12 Refers to experiments with organized urban living. Saltaire was founded by Sir Titus Salt, a manufacturer of alpaca woolens in England. Saltaire was established in 1853, partly as the result of his factory expansion. The town included educational and recreational centers, as well as almshouses and cooperative stores. George Pullman attempted a similar experiment 1880–1884 that ended with the famous Pullman Strike of 1894.

13 Kidder Peabody was a U.S.-based securities firm, established in Massachusetts in 1865. Its operations included investment banking, brokerage, and trading. The Firm was sold to the General Electric Corporation in 1986 and following heavy losses was subsequently sold to PaineWebber in 1994.

14 Wolfe, A. B. (of the University of Texas) (1920). Savers' surplus and interest rates. *Quarterly Journal of Economics, 35* (1), 1–35.

15 Herbert Joseph Davenport (1861–1931), economist with Austrian views at the University of Missouri. He completed his PhD in economics at Chicago in 1898 under Veblen, and taught there for many years before moving to Missouri and then Cornell.

16 Hugo Munsterberg (1863–1916) was a German-American psychologist and pioneer in applied psychology and industrial organization. Munsterberg began academic his career in Germany, but was wooed to Harvard temporarily (1882–1885) and then permanently in 1898.

17 Hartley Withers (1867–1950) was a financial journalist and author of popular economics books.

18 "Academic Socialism" refers to the state social policy advocated by a group of university professors, including Adolph Wagner, Gustav von Schmoller, and Werner Sombart.

19 "The Village Labourer: 1760–1832: A Study in the Government of England before the Reform Bill" by J.L. and Barbara Hammond. Originally published 1911, with a new edition in 1920. Henry Havelock Ellis (1859–1939) was a British physician and social reformer.

20 Herbert J. Davenport (1861–1931) studied in South Dakota, Harvard, Leipzig, and Paris before completing a PhD in economics under Veblen at the University of Chicago. He spent several years on staff there, before moving to the University of Missouri in 1908 and Cornell in 1916. Davenport made important contributions to tax theory, including an analysis of a single tax on land. For his repudiation of a single tax, see "Theoretical issues in the single tax," *American Economic Review, 7* (1), 1–30.

21 A threatened strike in 1918 by the Miners' Federation was narrowly adverted by the establishment of a Coal Industry Commission to review wages, hours, and the ownership of the industry in Great Britain. The commission was chaired by Justice Sankey, whose report proposed the nationalization of the mines. This suggestion was rejected by Parliament.

22 Richard Henry Tawney (1880–1962) was an English economic historian and social critic. In the *Acquisitive Society* (1921), he criticized contemporary society for its selfish individualism.